Donald Judd

Dietmar Elger (ed.)

Donald Judd Colorist

Hatje Cantz Publishers

7 Foreword

11 Introduction (to Don Judd, colorist)
Dietmar Elger

33 Donald Judd and the Endless Possibilities of Color
William C. Agee

53 Specific Objects – The Illusion of Factuality
Martin Engler

79 Some aspects of color in general and red and black in particular (1993)
Donald Judd

119 Biography

199 Solo Exhibitions

122 Bibliography

125 List of Exhibited Works

127 Lenders to the Exhibition

128 Colophon

129 Photo Credits

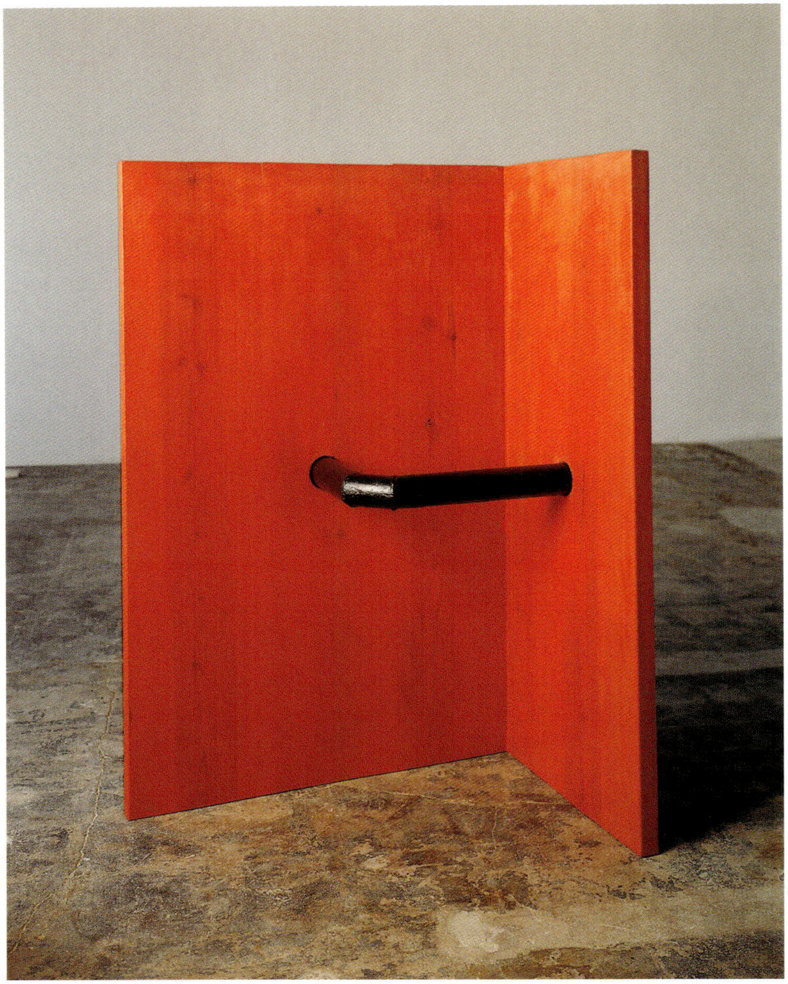

Untitled, 1962, oil on wood, enameled metal pipe, 48" x 33" x 21 1/2"

Foreword

Donald Judd is regarded as the leading representative of Minimal Art and as one of the most influential American artists in the 20th century. In his capacity as critic for various journals he initially wrote on the work of numerous contemporary artists, but later on he concentrated more on the question of art in general and its social context. He largely owes his status as one of the 20th century's few real artist-critics to the firm stance of his comments and the categorical sharpness of his judgements. Even when he was writing about other artists, Judd always related what he was saying to his own concept of art and the conditions of its production. For many younger artists, Donald Judd became a guiding light and a role model, in that he not only provided them with a vocabulary of forms that they could appropriate – citing or reworking what they found – but he also demonstrated through the consistency and confidence of his own attitude, how an artist may protect his or her work from the self-interest of the market, the exhibition circuit and the museums. In far-flung Marfa, Texas, he held up to the younger generation his own understanding of a proper way to deal with art. In the early 1960s, Donald Judd discovered a wholly innovative vocabulary of sculptural forms – with which he liberated himself from established notions of what a 'work' is. This step was such a radical break, above all with the European tradition, that he even suggested that rather than talking of sculpture any more, one could more accurately describe these works as specific objects. Sculpture was, in the truest sense of the word, toppled from its pedestal. Donald Judd placed his boxes directly on the floor in the exhibition space, and thus on a level with the viewer. Typically his works use industrial materials and a reduced vocabulary of forms, and in the process, classical composition gives way to a non-hierarchical treatment of the individual components of a work. The work in the studio is replaced by a manufacturing process that goes through a number of stages as in industrial production. The reception of Minimal Art has concentrated its discussions on these aspects and has exhaustively analyzed the perceptual qualities of the formal vocabulary of Minimalism. Meanwhile, Donald Judd himself was pointing towards other features in his own work: "Material, space, and color are the main aspects of visual art" were his opening words when he gave his 1993 lecture, "Some aspects of color in general and red and black in particular."

On the basis of this maxim, formulated by the artist himself, our exhibition aims to take a different, 'unused' look at Donald Judd's work, above all by concentrating on the question of color. Thus our attention is focused on an aesthetic quality which was, for Judd, equal in importance to the other two aspects of his art, but which has largely been ignored by critics. In a retrospective selection including over thirty objects made between 1962 and 1993, and a representative group of colored woodcuts, this exhibition demonstrates Judd's continuous and wide-ranging interest in color. Thus it becomes clear – particularly on the evidence of the exhibits from the nineties – that in his last years Donald Judd was starting to open up new, highly promising avenues for the use of color, although he was only able to realize a small number of these.

The exhibition *Donald Judd. Colorist* in the Sprengel Museum Hannover is in keeping with this institution's focus in its exhibitions and purchases on positions in Minimal Art and Post-Minimalism plus their reception by younger artists in the 1980s and 1990s. So far the Museum has been fortunate enough to acquire two works by Donald Judd for its permanent collection, one of which is a six-part wall piece on permanent loan from the HANNOVER Rück-Stiftung. Both of these works may be seen in the current exhibition.

This exhibition is of particular importance for the Kunsthaus Bregenz because the artist himself felt particularly drawn to the architecture and programs of this gallery and a number of joint projects with Bregenz were left unrealized on the artist's death. Amongst other things, Donald Judd designed an archive and library building for the Kunsthaus Bregenz – a simple, powerful piece of architecture, which (like his sculptures) is a logical and utterly clear development of its own construction, materials and proportions, at the same time providing for all the functions required of it (archive, administration, library, lecture theatre). This art-building is conceived as a unique, programmatic work, which would be deeply symbolic of the particular position that the Kunsthaus Bregenz occupies on the dynamic interface of art and architecture, which in itself goes hand in hand with an active interest in bringing together building construction and art. The detailed design for this project was a present from Donald Judd to the Kunsthaus, which, as an institution, now feels bound to honor this legacy. The current exhibition is a fitting opportunity to draw attention once again to this project, and to step up efforts to have these plans realized. For years any such attempts have been in vain.

Dietmar Elger both came up with the idea for *Donald Judd.*

Colorist and realized the exhibition. The project has been supported by the Artist's Estate right from the outset, which has also lent numerous works for the exhibition. For this, we are first and foremost immensely grateful to Rainer and Flavin Judd. The active involvement of Marianne Stockebrand, Director of the Chinati Foundation in Marfa, and Peter Ballantine of the Donald Judd Estate was crucial to the exhibition preparations and discussions surrounding the project. We owe a particular debt of gratitude to them for all their support. The artist's galleries, PaceWildenstein and Brooke Alexander in New York, Annemarie Verna in Zurich, Rolf Ricke in Cologne, and Lelong in Paris not only lent works for the exhibition but also kindly put us in touch with leading collectors. We should like to express our particular thanks to Douglas Baxter and Annemarie and Gianfranco Verna. And we should also like to thank most sincerely the museums that have lent us works, and all those private collectors who have so generously parted with works that they otherwise live with day by day.

We are fortunate indeed that William C. Agee – who curated the first Donald Judd exhibition in the Whitney Museum of American Art, New York – and Martin Engler agreed to contribute to the catalog with essays that approach the theme of the exhibition from distinctly different angles. In Hanover, the exhibition and the catalog have received generous financial backing from PreussenElektra, who have supported our work for many years now. We are deeply grateful to them. Lastly, we should like to thank all those who have worked on the exhibition in the two participating institutions for their untiring work during the preparations for the exhibition, and for their skill in smoothing the path toward its ultimate realization.

Ulrich Krempel
Sprengel Museum Hannover

Edelbert Köb
Kunsthaus Bregenz

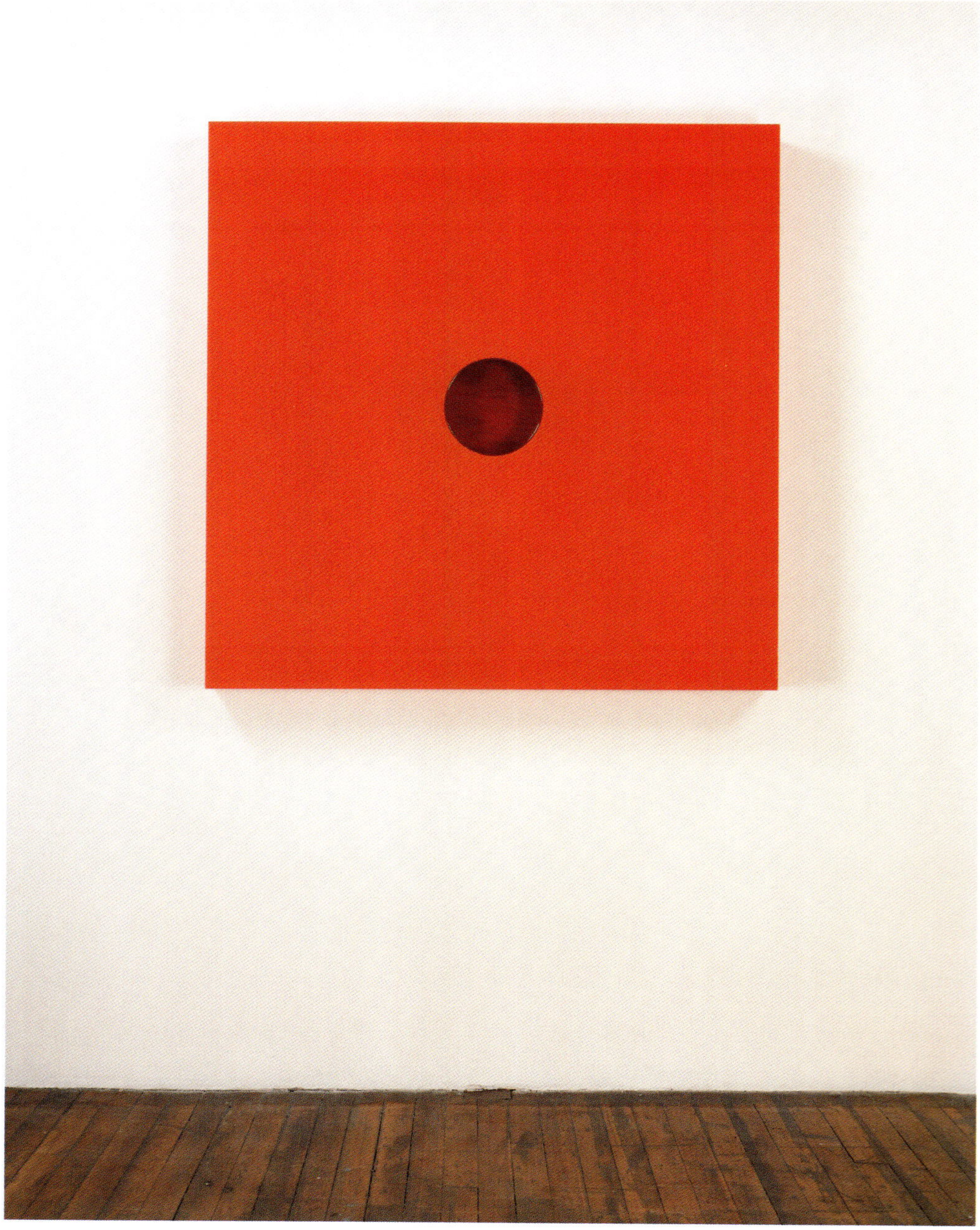

Untitled, 1962/1991, Douglas Fir plywood, painted, sand, glass, 46 1/2" x 46 1/2" x 4" (cat. no. 1)

Introduction (to Don Judd, colorist)

Dietmar Elger

The title of this exhibition and the accompanying publication owes its existence to a work by Dan Flavin. In 1987 Flavin made a group of neon-tube objects in five color combinations, namely pink with pink, red, yellow, blue and green. Each object is in the shape of a letter 'T' made out of four verticals standing on the floor with two tubes laid horizontally across the top of these. As ever, the artist left the work untitled, although he did dedicate it: "to Don Judd, colorist". A year earlier he had already made seven lithographs with the same title and printed in monochrome colors on gray, handmade paper. With this dedication from one artist to another, Dan Flavin was highlighting an aspect of Donald Judd's work that few had registered so far. In the context of the reception of Minimal Art, which was above all concerned with the issues surrounding reduced forms, the absence of composition and the presence of the material, the question of color and color-effects had been largely neglected for quite some time. The way that color primes objects with lyrical and atmospheric attributes, seemed hardly suitable for the rigorous formal language of Minimal Art, with the result that it was reduced by critics to no more than a means to distinguish different elements. Different color configurations made it possible to take a concept and to create a whole number of 'one-off' variants which were otherwise identical in terms of form and materials. This did, however, mean that color was stripped of its status as an aesthetic phenomenon and primarily employed in the service of a commercial marketing strategy.

In his critical writings and in numerous interviews Donald Judd repeatedly stressed his independence from Minimal Art. He most certainly did not want to be assigned to an artistic grouping which never existed as such. And at the same time he also repeatedly drew attention to the importance of color for his work[1] and granted it the same standing as the other two of the three most important constitutive elements of his art. In the essay *Some aspects of color in general and red and black in particular* (which is reprinted here on pp. 79–116), he starts by declaring his unshakeable belief in the importance of color: "Material, space and color are the main aspects of visual art."[2] Donald Judd supported this assertion with well-founded theoretical arguments, having made a detailed study of the use of color by artists ranging from Rogier van der Weyden, Titian and Henri Matisse to Josef Albers, Mark Rothko and Barnett Newman. In some of his late aluminum boxes from 1991 he even seems to be citing the stripes one associates with Barnett Newman, whose work he much admired (ill. p. 87). The black is concentrated here in a line, dividing the red color space in the centre.[3]

Since studying Philosophy and Art History at Columbia University in New York, Donald Judd had been familiar not only with the color theories of Johann Wolfgang von Goethe and M. E. Chevreul, but also with those of Adolf Hoelzel, Wassily Kandinsky and Josef Albers. Amongst other books, his own library included Albers' *Interaction of Color* in the lavish two-volume first edition of 1963 which Judd had reviewed (shortly after it appeared) in considerable detail in *Arts Magazine.*[4] In addition, his own collection contains several smaller paintings and works on paper by Josef Albers, and in his library in Marfa, Texas, there are also various other books on color perception such as David R. Hilbert's study *Color and Color Perception. A Study in Anthropocentric Realism* (1987), the *Histoire des Couleurs* by Manlio Brusatin (in a French translation of the Italian first edition of 1983), and three volumes of the *Designer's Guide to Color* (1984–1986), with practical instructions and examples of color combinations. The flap text on the dust wrapper of the first edition above all promotes the practical usefulness of the book: "In a broader sense, the book has real value to anyone who needs to confirm color ideas or to find color combinations, suggestions and examples presented in a straightforward, pure and neutral way."[5] Earlier on, when he was writing art criticism for a number of art journals (between 1959 and 1965), Judd had always homed in on the question of color, as in his review of sculptures by John Chamberlain, when he remarks: "Color is never unimportant, as it usually is in sculpture."[6] And even in an œuvre such as Andy Warhol's, which is so utterly dominated by the iconic presence of its famous motifs, Judd focused above all on the qualities of the colors and paints used: "The best thing about Warhol's work is the color," as he wrote in *Arts Magazine* on the occasion of the current exhibition by Warhol in the New York Stable Gallery in 1964: "The colors are often stained; they look like colored inks, and often black is stenciled over them, which produces a peculiar quality."[7]

For a long time there has been virtually no critical interest in color in Donald Judd's own work. It is only lately that there has any discussion of this subject. This exhibition and the accompanying catalog are intended therefore both to increase general awareness of this topic and to fuel the debate. It is true that, in 1968, William C. Agee was already pointing out the importance of color in Judd's work in the foreword to the catalog for Judd's first museum exhibition, which Agee himself put on in the Whitney Museum of American Art in New York. However, he then did not pursue this matter any further for many years. It was not until 1994 in the catalog for a posthumous exhibition at PaceWildenstein in New York that Agee once again put forward this view, and added to it.[8] Now, in this publication, William C. Agee – currently on the faculty of Hunter College in the City University, New York – broadens out this discussion and takes it a stage further (see pp. 33–51).

Donald Judd's late work in particular has helped initiate critical debate on the question of his use of color. In 1983 he was already making his multi-colored wall pieces in aluminum; in these pieces he succeeded in integrating color into his work in greater variety and complexity than ever before (ill. pp. 52–75). Above all in the early 90s he produced a number of works, such as the six-colored stack of 1992 (ill. p. 113) and the four-part yellow wall-piece from the year before (ill. p. 117), which now confronted the viewer with colored objects of an intensity that had not hitherto been seen in Judd's work. Rudi Fuchs, Director of the Stedelijk Museum Amsterdam, was referring in part to precisely these works when he stated that, "Over the years Donald Judd became ever more sure in what he did. In the last years of his life the colors became brighter than ever before. The pieces he was working on when he died indicated another brilliant development. There are one or two Cor-ten stackpieces of which the back of each of the boxes has a different color. He had not done that before."[9] In his essay for the catalog of the 1994 exhibition, *Donald Judd. The Moscow Installation* (at the Galerie Gmurzynska in Cologne), Fuchs confidently lauds Judd as a "Master of Color" – witness the title to his essay. As Fuchs sees it, Donald Judd's main interest as an artist was the problem of the colors of objects in space. He argues that the characteristically reduced forms of Minimal Art in Judd's work merely played a supporting role: "It was because he wanted to concentrate on articulating color in space, that he preferred these simple forms; they created spatial clarity in a more precise way than complex forms which attract too much attention for themselves."[10] Thus Rudi Fuchs draws a clear distinction in Judd's work between the leading role assigned to color and the accompanying part played by form. In late 1998 the Menil Collection in Houston even devoted an exhibition to this theme – the first of its kind. It was curated by Marianne Stockebrand, the Director of the Chinati Foundation in Marfa, and, with the title *Aspects of Color*, instigated yet another artistic dialogue between those long-standing friends, Dan Flavin and Donald Judd.

Donald Judd is regarded as the outstanding exponent of Minimal Art, as it became established in the mid-60s in New York. The other central figures are generally listed as Carl Andre, Dan Flavin, Robert Morris and Sol LeWitt, even if these artists never saw themselves as a group as such or appeared jointly in public

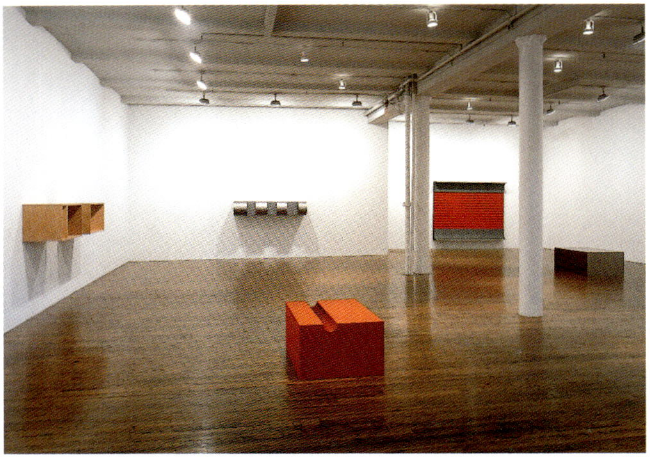

Installation, Paula Cooper Gallery, New York 1995

on their own initiative. The designation Minimal Art for that particular style had won the day against opposition from several alternatives – some even concurrent – such as ABC Art, Primary Structures or Cool Art. The term Minimal Art derives from an article of the same name by the English philosopher Richard Wollheim which appeared in *Arts Magazine* in 1965.[11] Wollheim sweepingly applied the term "Minimal Art" to examples of art from the last fifty years which could not be regarded as artworks in the traditional sense, in that they were either barely or not at all individual products by a specific artist. Wollheim discerned the roots of Minimal Art in Marcel Duchamp's readymades, his *Bottle Rack* of 1914 and his *Fountain* of 1917. Furthermore, Wollheim used the term Minimal Art in a somewhat derogatory manner, for in his view it described works which in fact only had a "minimal art content."[12] Even if this estimation has not held its ground and the definition of Minimal Art has undergone considerable change, nevertheless the criteria have remained indistinct and, depending on a person's point of view, have been applied to various other artists and, above all, to numerous painters.[13] Moreover, the even more general term Minimalism has extended the notion to apply to the most diverse of cultural phenomena and artistic genres, ranging from architecture and music to design and fashion.

For this reason – and entirely understandably – Donald Judd always argued vehemently against his work being claimed by Minimal Art. In his view, the term implied the existence of a group which had never been formed as such, it simplistically labeled artistic developments purely for publicity purposes, and it

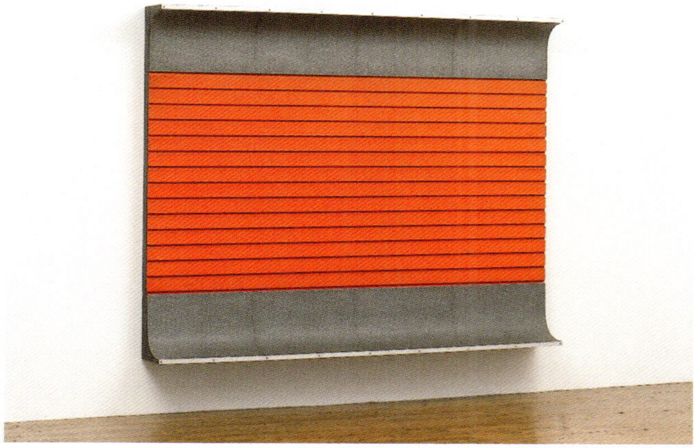

Untitled, 1963, oil on wood, galvanized iron and aluminum, 76" x 96" x 11 3/4"

was an unacceptable generalization. "The reality of it is that as a label 'Minimal Art' changed a great deal. Originally it meant three, four people, now it means half the world; there's been a great development in how many people are now part of this,"[14] as he complained in 1990 in a conversation with students at the Ruhr University in Bochum. On the same occasion he also underlined his own desire to be recognized as an individual artist with a specific body of work: "The artist wanted that and expected that; no-one expected to wind up in a category with a lot of other people and they resent that a great deal."[15] Without ignoring the singular achievements of each individual artist, works by Andre, Flavin, Judd, Morris and LeWitt are after all easy to identify and to tell apart for the practiced viewer, art historians are naturally interested precisely in these overall "categories", which help them to hold up an individual's œuvre as an exemplary artistic achievement within a particular epoch. As far as Minimal Art is concerned, art historians have formulated a few basic criteria which may be applied to Donald Judd's work: objects in Minimal Art operate with a vocabulary of forms that has been reduced to elementary, stereometric shapes. Taken together the individual units in a work make up simple arithmetical sequences and arrangements. In all of this, no single element is superior or inferior to any others. Thus the traditional criteria regarding composition and structural hierarchies are completely abandoned. The use of contemporary, technology-based materials such as aluminum, iron, zinc or neon tubes also distance these objects from artworks in bronze and marble. Moreover, when Minimal Artists were using these modern materials, they were also very consciously aiming to collaborate with the relevant, specialized industrial manufacturers. This step not only freed them from the isolation of the artist in his or her studio, but also established their artistic output as a societal process, which set in train a dialogue with a whole number of workers and technical experts. Donald Judd viewed this kind of activity above all as de-mystifying the artwork, and used it to take a stand against the traditions of European art history. In terms of contents, Minimal Art pieces refrain from any kind of instruction or information-giving. They take absolutely no account of political, social or psychological issues and questions from the outside world, but are wholly autonomous, and are defined purely by their relationship (in terms of form) to the surrounding space; they simply exist as objects in this world. Their equal right to membership in the world of their recipients is reinforced by the fact that they do without pedestals, which means that rather than setting up their own system of references, they position themselves on a 'base' which they share with their viewers. Now visitors and exhibits have equal rights in the same space and on the same floor. Unlike sculpture, painting – in Judd's view – can never achieve this, because it creates illusions and can only suggest mass and volume. Consequently he was persistently dissatisfied with his paintings right through the 50s and into the early 60s. In 1965 he came back to this basic problem of painting once again: "Except for a complete and unvaried field of color or marks, anything spaced in a rectangle and on a plane suggests something in and on something else, something in its surround, which suggests an object or figure in its space, in which these are clearer instances of a similar world – that's the main purpose of painting."[16] In making this comment, Donald Judd was criticizing any kind of illusionism, including efforts to disguise the actual conditions and qualities of the materials, mass, color and/or construction of an artwork.

The earliest work in this exhibition, conceived in 1962 (although only executed a great deal later) already goes some way to solving the problems that Judd, the painter, had with flat picture surfaces (ill. p. 10). This work consists of a square with sides that are over a meter in length. With a depth of ten centimeters it looks like a box and creates an object-like effect. The circular hole cut into the centre of the surface again draws attention to the depth of the piece and at the same time underlines the fact that this work is, in some senses, an object. At the same time Judd uses the cylindrical hole as an example of the way in which space creates color, in that the red paint has the glow of a dark-toned color space. The pane of glass fulfills two, apparently contradictory, functions. On one hand, it makes a smooth front for the square surface, on the other hand the glass pane is perceived as a real object and thus also as an anti-illusionistic fragment of reality (as an *objet trouvé*). Donald Judd also underlines the 'objecthood' of the work in that it is painted – in the cadmium red that he favored at the time – not only on the front but also on the sides. As well as this, he mixed the paint with sand which means that the surface is somewhat rough and tactile. Thus the viewer's perception of this untitled work switches constantly between a red picture-surface and a relief-like object on the wall. As Donald Judd himself put it in his essay *Specific Objects* in 1965: "Three dimensions are real space. That gets rid of the problem of illusionism and of literal space, space in and around marks and colors – which is riddance of one of the salient and most objectionable relics of European art. The several limits of painting are no longer present. A work can be as powerful as it can be thought to be. Actual space is intrinsically more powerful and specific than paint on a flat surface."[17]

Judd had already drawn the logical consequences of these observations for his own work three years earlier, in his drawings for boxes (1962). At the time he only realized three possible versions and did not take them up again until the late 80s. These include the untitled object of 1962/87 (ill. p. 18). It stands directly on the floor, that is to say, relies neither on a pedestal nor on any factual or conceptual demarcation between itself and the surrounding space. It is a right-angled cube made of plywood and painted evenly in cadmium red. This was Judd's preferred color for his objects at the time (although not to the exclusion of all others), and he repeatedly returned to it. Cadmium red light seemed to him, in the early 60s, to be the ideal color to really bring out the actual shape of the objects. At the same time, cadmium red imbued the objects with a vibrant optical presence in the space. In a lengthy and informative interview with John Coplans in 1971, Judd spoke about his preference for this color over all other colors: "I like the color and I like the quality of cadmium red light. And then also, I thought for a color it had the light value for a three-dimensional object. If you paint something black or any dark color, you can't tell what its edges are like. If you paint it white, it seems small and purist. And the red, other than a gray of that value, seems to be the only color that really makes an object sharp and defines its contours and angles."[18]

Another striking feature of this exhibit from 1962/87 is the semicircular incision into the top of the object, which runs parallel to the long edge along the entire length of the surface. And yet, this is by no means an attempt on Judd's part to break down or divide the composition of the closed block. Rather the incision fulfills the anti-illusionism that Judd required of his works. For the opening allows the viewer to see inside the object and its three, evenly spaced partitions. In this way the actual construction of the object is plain for all to see, the strength of the material is perfectly evident, and nothing is concealed from the viewer. For Donald Judd this openness in his objects was not merely a technical ploy but above all an integral part of the concept of the work.

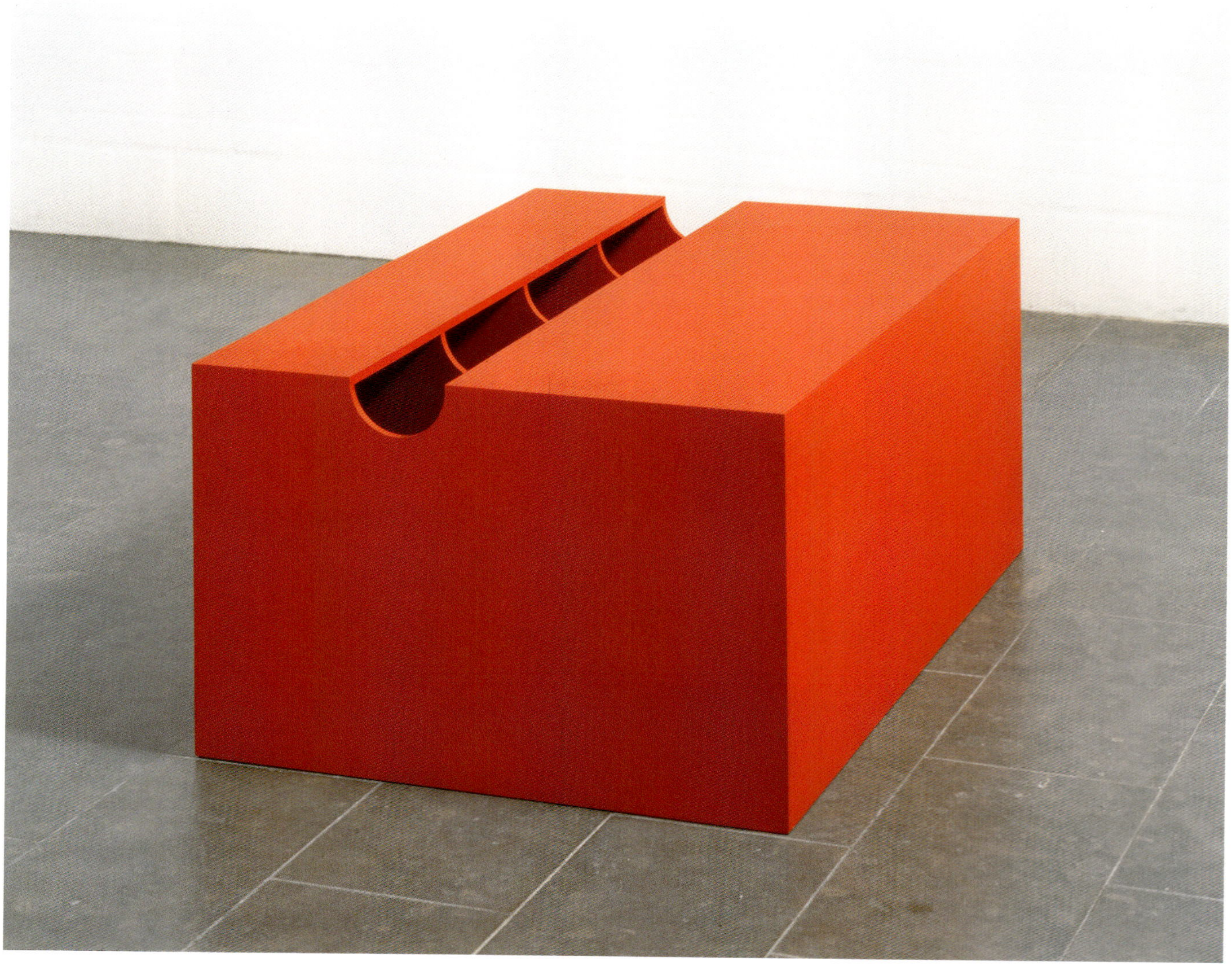

Untitled, 1962/1987, Douglas Fir plywood, painted, 19 1/2" x 45" x 30 1/2" (cat. no. 2)

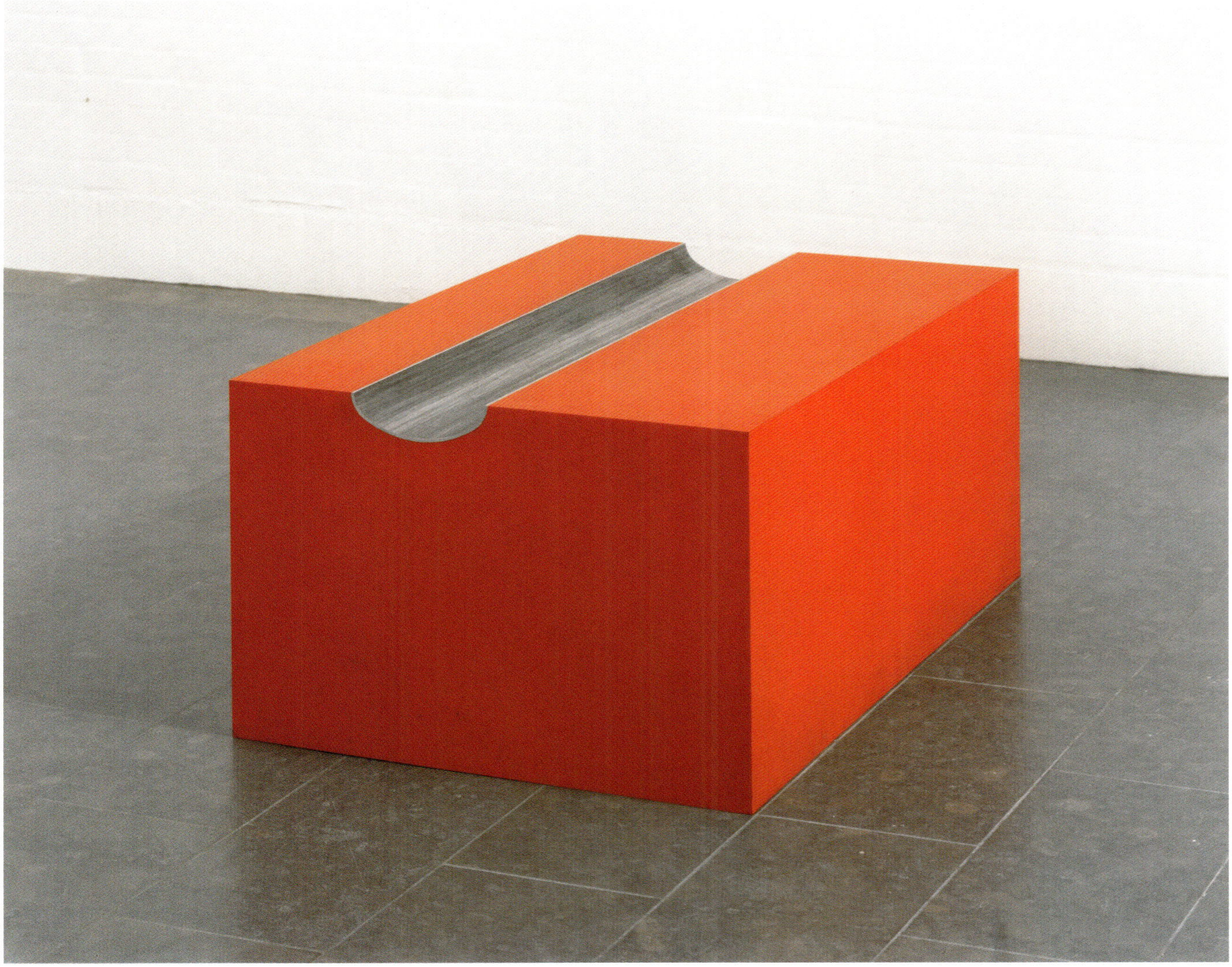

Untitled, 1968/1991, Douglas Fir plywood, painted, aluminum, 19 1/2" x 45" x 30 1/2" (cat. no. 4)

Although Judd was once again making numerous plywood pieces in the late 60s, at the time he felt that this material was too much bound up with a particular craft process and, as such, too much a part of traditional art history. The changeover to various metals, such as aluminum, iron and steel, offered a way out of this, and simultaneously solved a whole number of problems. Using metals – aluminum was still a very new material at the time – not only freed the artist from art-historical traditions but also meant that art production shifted from its familiar studio situation into the realms of modern manufacturing. The metal sheets were also significantly thinner than the plywood; thus the hollow spaces in the objects seemed much more logical to the viewer in the light of the qualities of the materials used. Above all they allowed the artist to work with much greater precision and – another major advantage over plywood as far as Judd was concerned – he did not have to paint the metal surface, since they already had their own intrinsic color. Donald Judd could hardly be completely satisfied with the cadmium red, plywood boxes in that the painted finish prevented the viewer from identifying the material, or at least made it harder. Consequently all the later plywood pieces were left untreated, and the graining of the wood was accepted as an integral part of the material. In view of Judd's insistence that his own work should be anti-illusionistic, this was a wholly logical move.

For Donald Judd, color always occupied a central position in his approach to art, whether in his research into different color theories, in the work of his role-models in art history, or in his own praxis. Having succeeded in 1962 in liberating his works from wall-surfaces and in overcoming pictoriality, he then took what he had learnt in these different areas, and applied it to his work with color in space. He once summed up his conclusions as follows: "My thought comes from painting even if I don't paint."[19] However, at the same time, Judd was forced to recognize that he was setting out into artistic terra incognita almost entirely on his own: "There is a history of color in art. Every other generation has a new idea of color. However, this is a generation without ideas. At the present space and color have in common complete neglect."[20] As he saw it, in an ideal situation the color would be in the material, that is to say, identical with the material. It was only by this means that he could avoid any kind of illusionism – such as was still present in the early painted plywood pieces. As he himself put it in the catalog for his exhibition at the Staatliche Kunsthalle in Baden-Baden in 1989, "I don't like plain plywood or plain concrete or plain metal to be considered without color. So to me they are colored. But I also know that at least it's not bright color, it's not red and blue. So it is a pretty big span. But it's best to consider everything as color."[21] Thus he valued the color of the silvery gleam of the aluminum, the shifting shimmer of the galvanized iron, the warm gold-tones of brass, the matt red-brown of Cor-ten steel and the gray of the concrete works.

Despite the variety of materials – and the gradations within that variety which came from the different treatments – the actual spectrum of colors available was limited, and intense colors were simply not to be had.

However, since color occupied a central position for Donald Judd in his work, and he also wanted to be dealing with strong color contrasts, he decided to make a concession and to paint the metal, albeit only too well aware that this could only ever be a compromise on his part, and, as he put it, only ever a second choice.[22] Thus he chose to apply the paint preferably by those methods which at least allowed him to retain the authentic surface of the metal. These included anodizing, galvanizing, and enameling. Another option open to him was to use metallic motor-cycle paint from Harley-Davidson (ill. pp. 29, 30). This paint could be applied immensely thinly, allowing the surface of the metal to shine through. Moreover, the metallic finish corresponds to the metal surface of the material itself. Donald Judd had come across this paint in 1963 through John Chamberlain, who was already using it to paint his sculptures. The following year Judd discovered another material – plexiglass – which would open up a whole range of new possibilities. Almost more than any other material, plexiglass lived up to Judd's stipulation that material and color should form a single entity, for color is truly inherent in plexiglass. It is available in an almost endless variety of factory-made colors, and can, in addition, be opaque or transparent, dull, intensely glowing or even fluorescent. The object, *Untitled* (1966; ill. p. 28), is a fine example of some of the possibilities that this material offered to Judd. It is a closed cube made of plexiglass with side-walls of high-grade steel. The surfaces of both these two different materials display the same, factory-finish smoothness. The amber-colored plexiglass is transparent and reveals the interior of the cube and how it is constructed. The viewer can clearly make out four wires holding the side-walls together. In this work the transparent plexiglass allows Donald Judd to achieve the openness he had already been striving for in the early box of 1962, but now without having to impair the smooth surface with any kind of incision.

With his first free-standing objects in 1962, Donald Judd liberated himself from the wall and thus from pictorial associations, too. Over the years he repeatedly pledged his allegiance to sculpture as a medium and in a conversation in 1990 once again made this point: "One reason I didn't like to make painting but like three-dimensional work so much is because I like space a great deal."[23] Nevertheless Judd was not minded to entirely give up the wall as a location for his art to operate in. Yet he could only return his objects to the wall with any success if he were at the same time to exclude any kind of illusionism or pictorial elements. Through his detour via the cadmium red boxes he found solutions which he would probably never have arrived at by yet further reducing his painting. His so-called progressions, which he started to make in

1964, initially in varnished wood, were a direct result of his work on floor pieces. Judd once again turned to semi-circular forms (which were in fact simply the left-overs from his plywood boxes), and mounted these horizontally on the walls as objects in their own right. Very soon he changed to using metal, integrated colors, varied the forms and thus developed a number of different groups of progressions (ill. pp. 25, 29, 37). The crucial point was that these new works, unlike the wall pieces of 1962, had an extremely condensed appearance and thus presented the viewer with virtually no surfaces where illusions of space might have arisen. In terms of their forms, it was again important to Judd to shun traditional principles of composition. With this in mind, he came up with two options that he returned to again and again throughout the rest of his career as an artist: one option was to choose identical sub-elements, whereby the individual units would be exactly the same size and shape and the distances between them would also be constant. These objects are symmetrical but not put together according to any hierarchy. In other works he did choose an asymmetrical structure, but in order to again avoid having to contend with hierarchies and composition, he would choose different kinds of progressions.

One sequence that he frequently used – consisting of a number of units and intervening spaces – was constructed according to the following pattern: $\underline{11} + 1 + \underline{6} + 2 + \underline{3} + 3 + \underline{2} + 6 + \underline{1}$ (underlinings indicate physical units as opposed to spaces). This, at first sight, baffling sequence of numbers does, however, conceal a whole number of logical inter-connections. The first distance (1) corresponds to the last unit ($\underline{1}$) – as though it were cut out from one position and repositioned at the end of the object. The next element ($\underline{6}$) corresponds similarly to the penultimate space, and so on. The middle elements (6 + 3 + 2, or 2 + 3 + 6) add up to the length of the first element (11). The first two elements (11 + 1), added together, are exactly the same length as the four last ones (3 + 2 + 6 + 1). In the interview with John Coplans, Judd himself pointed out more possible progressions (which he had used in his work), plus their effects on viewers: "In one of the progressions I used the Fibonacci series. In another I used the kind of inverse natural number series: one, minus a half, plus a third, a fourth, a fifth etc. No one other than a mathematician is going to know what that series really is. You don't walk up to it and understand how it is working, but I think you do understand that there is a scheme there, and that it doesn't look as if it is just done part by part visually. So it's not conceived part by part, it's done in one shot. The progressions made it possible to use an asymmetrical arrangement, yet to have some sort of order not involved in composition."[24] In the so-called Fibonacci series mentioned by Judd, and which is named after its discoverer, Leonardo Fibonacci (a mathematician and philosopher in thirteenth century Italy), each number is generated by adding together the two previous numbers, i.e., 1 + 1 + 2 + 3 + 5 + 8 + 13

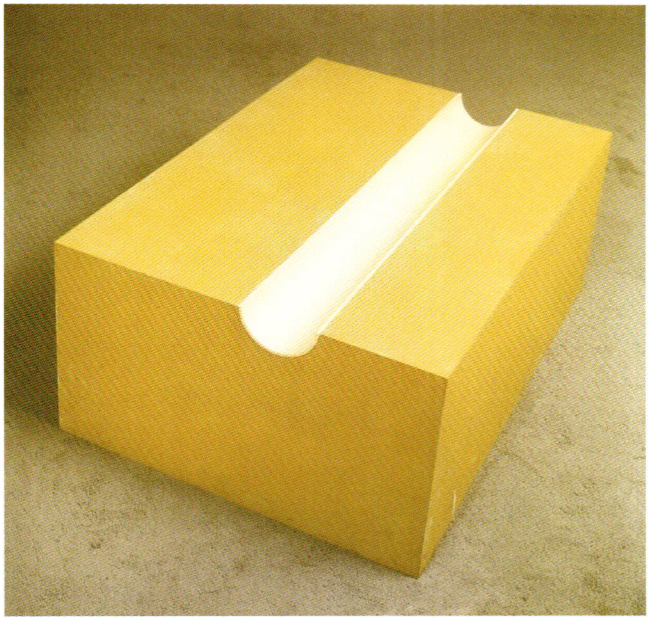

Untitled, 1964, oil on wood, enameled iron, 19 1/2" x 48" x 34"

+ 21 etc. Even if the viewer cannot recognize and decode these progressions, that is to say the structures in his works, nevertheless he will intuitively sense that the objects have not been arranged according to some subjective compositional plan, but that they follow an objective, internal logic.

In a radio interview, which the journalist Bruce Glaser conducted as early as February 1964 with Frank Stella and Donald Judd, the latter responded to a question about his rejection of compositional effects: "Well, those effects tend to carry with them all the structures, values, feelings of the whole European tradition. It suits me fine if that's all down the drain."[25] This outspoken criticism of the traditions of art in Europe, from which Judd expressly distanced himself in his work, comes up repeatedly in his statements. While the paintings of the Abstract Expressionists – as in the early works of Jackson Pollock, Mark Rothko and Barnett Newman – still retained important influences from European émigrés, Donald Judd was seeking to leave European art history behind him, and to instigate a new beginning, freed from past traditions. And it was specifically pictorial composition and illusion that he identified as the two central criteria that persisted throughout the evolution of art right down to the present day. In his view, these two features were so intricately bound up in tradition that only a radical break could lead to a new kind of innovative, contemporary art. Although Judd frequently attacked European art of the past, it was never his intention to confront it with American contemporary art, freed of all historical constraints. Europe merely served him as a synonym for all painting and sculpture that was locked into its own traditions.

Judd's innovation in terms of form also imply moral aspirations. The anti-compositional principle of the progressions and his sequences of equal-status elements abolish any form of hierarchy, and establish an egalitarian principle in which no one individual element may be set above or below any others. Independently of their position within a holistic object, each element claims the same value as the others. The other main principle in Judd's approach to his work may aptly be described as a striving for openness. All the decisions he has to make during the production of the work are geared toward openness: the form should be as clear as possible, reduced, and it should make sense to the recipient. The materials are openly displayed and should be recognizable for their own intrinsic qualities. Above all, when Judd was painting objects, it was important to him to retain these qualities, and he chose his materials accordingly. Transparent panes of plexiglass, incisions and hollow spaces reveal the internal structures of the works, with the result that nothing is hidden from the viewer, and the art cannot shroud itself in mystery. In the joint interview with Bruce Glaser, Frank Stella came up with a fitting formulation for this anti-illusionism: "What you see, is what you see."[26] This premise is just as appropriate for our perception of Judd's work. Even the form and colors on sections of a work not visible to the viewer can be deduced by the viewer on the basis of the reduced, logical structure of each object. Reliability, confirmation and the avoidance of surprise effects are amongst the main experiences that viewers have in their contemplation of Donald Judd's art: the objects in the arrangement are all the same size, the distances between them are identical (corresponding to the depth of the box from the front to the partition), the first impression, that this work is made of aluminum, is confirmed on closer observation; the construction process is evident from the unconcealed screws, and as one walks round the boxes, it becomes clear that the partition on the central axis that one sees from the back of the boxes is identical to the partition one sees from the front (ill. p. 44).

However, the fact that any contemplation of Donald Judd's art nevertheless brings with it endlessly new, lasting experiences, must be due to the interplay between the reduction of the compositional elements and the complexity of their interconnections: "Most art, including mine, involves several things at once, none developed toward exclusivity. Art is generally more specific than it used to be; its visible aspects are more important; but usually there is a comparative balance between the few main aspects"[27]

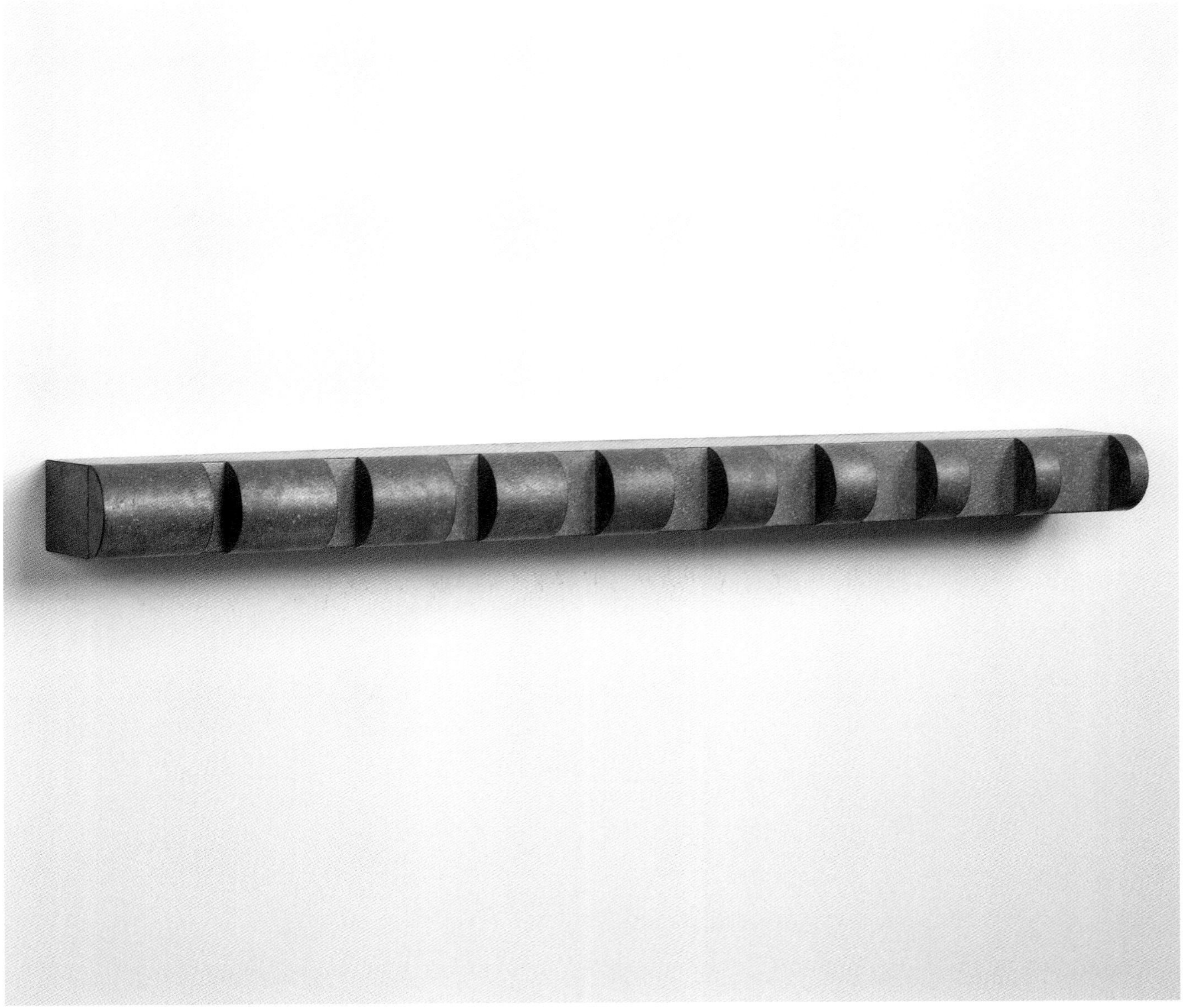

Untitled, 1969, galvanized iron, 5" x 69" x 8 1/2" (cat. no. 5)

– Donald Judd writing in 1969 in a catalog essay for a Dan Flavin exhibition, explaining the relationship between the individual elements that go to make up a work, and the viewer's perception of them as a whole. Thus Judd puts form, materials, structure and color all on an equal footing and uses them in the reduced manner already described. In their totality, however, and in their interplay, they open up a completely new level of multiplicity and complexity. And, at the same time, the totality of the work leads to visual responses that are far greater than the sum of the individual materials and processes, and which can engender a deeply affecting optical sensation. In his realization of the work, Judd juxtaposes its various qualities. The dull, light-absorbent surface of the Cor-ten plates is set against the glowing red of the reflective plexiglass panes, the raw metal surface against the anodized aluminum – and then there is the complex interplay of color contrasts of the aluminum pieces (from 1983 onwards), and the unsettling dissolution of the materiality of the late 1993 stack (ill. p. 109), where the reflective copper surfaces make the individual elements seem transparent, just as though the viewer could look right through the boxes. In a small number of objects Judd laid one plexiglass pane on top of the other, which created unusual new color effects not available in the plexiglass straight from the factory (ill. pp. 86, 88, 89). In other works he took advantage of the reflective qualities of paint. The 1971, open-topped, copper cube in the collection of the London Tate Gallery is only painted red on the inside of the base; nevertheless the color glows with such an intensity that it seems to fill the entire interior space, and the viewer approaching from afar already perceives the color as a diffuse, red haze floating above the object (ill. p. 40).

In 1989, Donald Judd came back to this effect with his large format aluminum boxes, two of which are on display in this exhibition (ill. pp. 94–97). The interior sections in blue and black aluminum, and above all the blue plexiglass base of the first object, bounce the daylight back as colored light onto the side walls of the boxes. In the case of these objects, which Judd made along with ten other variants for an installation in the Staatliche Kunsthalle, Baden-Baden, this effect was carefully calculated. However, in a conversation with the curator of the exhibition, Jochen Poetter, Judd made the following comment on this colored-light effect: "I only planned on one. The blue one I knew about. I knew the blue would do that. But I didn't think about the others in that way. So that's pretty, it's free like light."[28] In these remarks Judd introduces a category into the evaluation of his own work which had been completely absent from his earlier statements, as from the reception of Minimal Art as a whole.[29] In view of the desired all-embracing neutrality of their objects, *beauty* of any kind had never been a suitable criterion by which to assess either Donald Judd's art or that of Carl Andre, Dan Flavin, Sol LeWitt or Robert Morris either. Still, it should not be regarded as equal in importance to the formal language and materials used in a piece, but rather as a quality of the effects and the interplay of form, materials, surfaces and, above all, of color. Unlike these four aspects, which may be regarded as concerned with the perception of the object, beauty is dependent on how the object is experienced, and thus open to manipulation by subjective influences. On the other hand, one of the outstanding achievements of Donald Judd's art is that, in his work, he never flinched from this (dangerous) aesthetic category, yet at the same time always succeeded in serenely navigating his way past the threatening cliffs of mere decoration.

Judd's interest in color is closely connected with his mention of 'beauty' as an attribute that could be used as a criterion in viewing his art. With the group of horizontal, sheet-aluminum wall pieces begun in 1983, where he uses a whole number of colors, this interest took on greater importance. Here color takes on a leading, creative role. Judd used open aluminum boxes in three different formats (30, 60 and 90 cm), and screwed them together to create objects up to 450 cm in length. In addition he made a number of wall pieces – some high, some two-part (ill. pp. 60, 61, 63, 65) – as well as a total of seven free-standing monumental containers out of identical, large aluminum units (each 150 cm long) (ill. pp. 52, 74). For this group, Judd chose exclusively boldly colored gloss paints, which were enameled into the material by means of a relatively complicated process. Where he had previously concentrated on a maximum of two colors, now he put together complex, strongly contrasting color combinations, generally in multiples of two (4, 6, 8 etc.). In doing so, he was careful to distribute the colors so that no adjacent units were in the same shade. He continued to work on the group, and by the late 80s was starting to concentrate on a smaller number of colors, allowing these to extend across a number of elements screwed together, or even to cover the entire front of a wall piece with an intense, monochrome plane. In his selection of colors Judd was now picking combinations that were as neutral as possible. He neither wanted to allude to art-historical forebears nor to his own earlier work. He similarly steered clear of color sequences that are loaded with some symbolic meaning. An object in black, red and gold or in the colors of the tricolor would have been completely out of the question. Even a straightforwardly harmonic combination was something he expressly wished to avoid, even if he did not always manage to resist them in practice. In his lengthy essay, *Some aspects of color in general and red and black in particular* of 1993, he described the thinking behind his choice of colors for the aluminum pieces as follows: "In the sheet-aluminum works I wanted to use more and diverse bright colors than before. As I will describe later, there are many combinations, some old as I listed, and some my own from earlier work. I wanted to avoid both of these. I especially didn't want the combinations to be harmonious, an old and im-

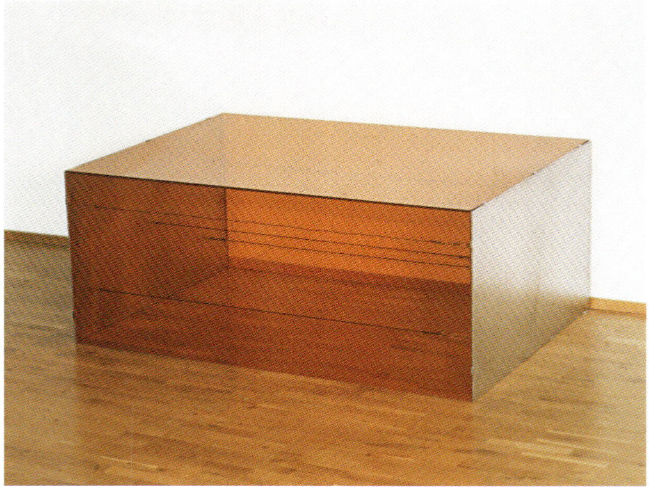

Untitled, 1966, stainless steel, plexiglass, 20" x 48" x 34"

plicative idea, which is the easiest to avoid, or to be inharmonious in reaction, which is harder to avoid. I wanted all of the colors to be present at once. I didn't want them to combine. I wanted a multiplicity all at once that I had not known before. This was very difficult."[30]

While he strove for autonomy in his artworks, Judd always defended them against being commandeered for any kind of extra-artistic ideas or tasks: "As I said before, the art is a whole thing in itself. It's not a medium for something else, so it's not teaching. It's not a moral thing, it's not an ethical thing, it's not a scientific thing; it's art. It's not about something else; it's about itself and its own qualities."[31] Judd, who was a very political artist and who also allowed these ideas to percolate into his theoretical statements,[32] nevertheless always separated his objects from his views on politics and society. In an interview Judd once cited the work of Hans Haacke as the antithesis in this respect to his own approach. While he made it clear that he sympathized with the political sentiments Haacke was expressing in his work, he nonetheless found the work itself not entirely convincing.[33]

Both before Judd and since Judd there have been many other twentieth century artists who shared his attitude. Ad Reinhardt put it extremely succinctly in 1958: "Art is art and everything else is everything else."[34] At the same time, however, these artists recognized the contradictions in their position, for precisely those things which claimed to be apolitical were in themselves a political statement. In 1995, Felix Gonzalez-Torres eluci-

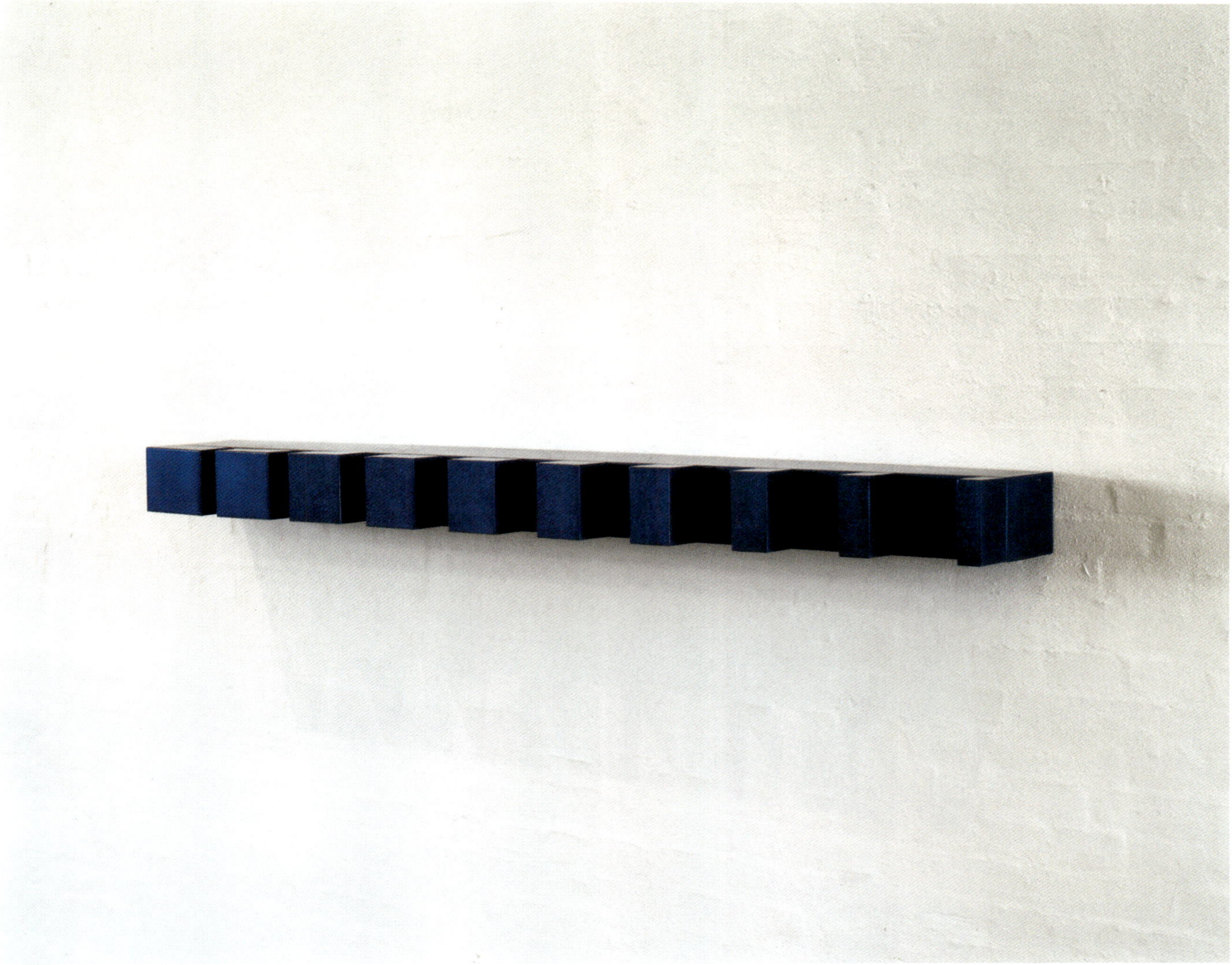

Untitled, 1968, lacquer on galvanized iron, 5" x 69" x 9" (cat. no. 3)

dated this conundrum in an interview with Robert Storr: "Let's look at abstraction and let's consider the most successful of those political artists, Helen Frankenthaler. Why are they the most successful artists, even more than Kosuth, much more than Hans Haacke, much more than Nancy (Spero) and Leon (Golub) or Barbara Kruger. Because they don't look political!"[35] In response to the Vietnam War, in 1970 the journal *Artforum* sent out a questionnaire in which they asked what form political activity by artists ought to take. In his answer, Donald Judd once again declared his feelings of personal political responsibility, but staunchly rejected the idea that his work should be used as a political instrument. At the same time, however, he did credit the supposedly apolitical art of the 60s with hidden, socially destructive powers: "I suspect one reason for the popularity of American art is that the museums and the collectors didn't understand it enough to realize that it was against much in the society."[36]

As early as 1923, Kurt Schwitters – the Merz artist from Hanover – had expressed the hope that, precisely because of its distance from the actual course of events, art might exercise a political influence on society: "But art doesn't have anything to do with things outside of art, so not with war either. But were art to consistently position itself alongside the evils of this world, then a beneficial influence might possibly flow from it into our culture."[37] Schwitters' idealism was of course imbued with notions of salvation and world-improving utopias, of the kind that had sprung up all over Europe in the wake of the First World War. But we find a trace of this hope lingering in statements by Donald Judd: "I have definite political opinions and to some extent they are more developed than other people's and some other artists' too. That's got to be in there I guess."[38] Judd's works affect society by virtue of their role as potential models. The openness that Judd always required of his art is more than just a category describing the way an artist handles structures, materials, surfaces and colors: it has its roots in the underlying morals of the artist. In the sense that these objects cannot be deployed as instruments of some kind – neither trying to hide things nor to delude their viewers – demonstrates that their very openness is also a form of *honesty*. And this is what gives Donald Judd's art a moral status. The objects serve as models that society may take note of. With the openness of their forms, with their demonstration of honesty, they may provide the viewer with an example that he may recognize as a desirable model for his own doing and thinking.

From the German by Fiona Elliott

Notes

1 Cf. Donald Judd and John Griffiths, *Donald Judd* (interview), in *New York New Art, Art and Design*, London 1989, p. 48; Donald Judd et al., *Discussion with Donald Judd* (Interview), in *Donald Judd* (cat.), Kunstverein St. Gallen, 1990, pp. 44–45.

2 Donald Judd, *Some aspects of color in general and red and black in particular*, (Speech held on the occasion of the award ceremony for the Sikkens Foundation Prize, on 27 November 1993 in the Stedelijk Museum Amsterdam), Sikkens Foundation, Sassenheim/Stedelijk Museum Amsterdam, 1993. In this volume: p. 79.

3 Cf.: William C. Agee, *Donald Judd in Retrospect: An Appreciation*, in *Donald Judd. Sculpture* (cat.), PaceWildenstein Gallery, New York 1994, p. 11.

4 Cf.: Donald Judd, *Books. Arts Magazine* (November 1963), *Interaction of Color by Josef Albers* (book review), in *Complete Writings 1959–1975*, Halifax/New York 1975, p. 102.

5 *Designer's Guide to Color,* vol. I, San Francisco 1994, Jacket. Judd received the first two volumes as presents from his children Rainer and Flavin. Each title page has the handwritten inscription: "R + F 25 Dec 85".

6 Quoted in Donald Judd, *John Chamberlain* (1965), in *John Chamberlain. New Sculpture* (cat.), The Pace Gallery, New York 1989, p. V.

7 Donald Judd, *Andy Warhol* (exhibition review), in *Complete Writings 1959–1975*, Halifax/New York 1975, p. 70.

8 William C. Agee, *Donald Judd in Retrospect: An Appreciation,* in *Donald Judd. Sculpture* (cat.), PaceWildenstein Gallery, New York 1994, pp. 5–17.

9 Rudi Fuchs, *Master of Colour,* in *Donald Judd. The Moscow Installation* (cat.), Galerie Gmurzynska, Cologne 1994, p. 11.

10 Rudi Fuchs, *Master of Colour,* in *Donald Judd. The Moscow Installation* (cat.), Galerie Gmurzynska, Cologne 1994, p. 10.

11 Richard Wollheim, *Minimal Art*, in *Arts Magazine* (January 1965).

12 Richard Wollheim, *Minimal Art (1965)*, in *Minimal Art. A Critical Anthology*, New York 1968, p. 387.

13 Cf. Gregory Battcock (ed.), *Minimal Art. A Critical Anthology*, New York 1968; Kenneth Baker, *Minimalism. Art of Circumstance*, New York 1988; Frances Colpitt, *Minimal Art. The Critical Perspective*, Seattle 1990; Gregor Stemmrich (ed.), *Minimal Art. Eine kritische Retrospektive*, Dresden/Basel 1995; David Batchelor, *Minimalism. Movements in Modern Art*, London 1997. Of the publications listed here only the study by David Batchelor concentrates exclusively on the original group consisting of Andre, Flavin, Judd, Morris and LeWitt. All the others include additional artists in their surveys of Minimalism – above all Frank Stella, Robert Ryman, Tony Smith, Jo Baer and Brice Marden.

14 Donald Judd et al., *Discussion with Donald Judd* (interview), in *Donald Judd* (cat.), Kunstverein St. Gallen, 1990, p. 50.

15 Donald Judd et al., *Discussion with Donald Judd* (interview), in *Donald Judd* (cat.), Kunstverein St. Gallen, 1990, p. 50.

16 Donald Judd, *Specific Objects (1965)*, in *Complete Writings 1959–1975*, Halifax/New York 1975, p. 182.

17 Donald Judd, *Specific Objects (1965)*, in *Complete Writings 1959–1975*, Halifax/New York 1975, p. 184.

18 Donald Judd and John Coplans, *Don Judd* (interview), in *Don Judd* (cat.), Pasadena Art Museum, Pasadena 1971. Reprinted in *Donald Judd* (cat.), Centro Cultural de Belém, 1997, p. 28.

19 Quoted in William C. Agee, *Donald Judd in Retrospect: An Appreciation,* in *Donald Judd. Sculpture* (cat.), PaceWildenstein Gallery, New York 1994, p. 12.

20 Donald Judd, *Some aspects of color in general and red and black in particular (1993).* In this volume: p. 91.

21 Donald Judd and Jochen Poetter, *Back to Clarity. Interview with Donald Judd* (interview), in *Donald Judd* (cat.), Staatliche Kunsthalle Baden-Baden, 1989, p. 94.

22 Cf. Donald Judd et al., *Discussion with Donald Judd,* in *Donald Judd* (cat.), Kunstverein St. Gallen, 1990, p. 54.

23 Donald Judd et al., *Discussion with Donald Judd*, in *Donald Judd* (cat.), Kunstverein St. Gallen, 1990, p. 55.

24 Donald Judd and John Coplans, *Don Judd* (interview), in *Don Judd* (cat.), Pasadena Art Museum, Pasadena 1971. Reprinted in Donald Judd (cat.), Centro Cultural de Belém, 1997, p.38.

25 Donald Judd, Frank Stella and Bruce Glaser, *Questions to Stella und Judd (1964)*, in Gregory Battcock (ed.), *Minimal Art. A Critical Anthology,* New York 1968, p. 150.

26 Donald Judd, Frank Stella and Bruce Glaser, *Questions to Stella and Judd (1964),* in Gregory Battcock (ed.), *Minimal Art. A Critical Anthology*, New York 1968, p. 158.

27 Donald Judd, *Aspects of Flavin's Work* (1969, exhibition review), in *Complete Writings 1959–1975*, Halifax/New York 1975, p. 199.

28 Donald Judd and Jochen Poetter, *Back to Clarity. Interview with Donald Judd*, in *Donald Judd* (cat.), Staatliche Kunsthalle Baden-Baden, 1989, p. 99.

29 Only two authors, Jochen Poetter (briefly) and Rudi Fuchs (in more detail) discuss the importance of beauty in Donald Judd's work. Cf.: Jochen Poetter, *Hermetic and Open – Precision and Beauty. Donald Judd at the Kunsthalle Baden-Baden,* in *Donald Judd* (cat.), Staatliche Kunsthalle Baden-Baden, 1989, p. 48; Rudi Fuchs, *Decent Beauty,* in *Kunst + Design. Donald Judd. Preisträger der Stankowski-Stiftung 1993* (cat.), Museum Wiesbaden, 1993, pp. 83–84.

30 Donald Judd, *Some aspects of color in general and red and black in particular (1993).* In this volume: p. 114.

31 Donald Judd and Jochen Poetter, *Back to Clarity. Interview with Donald Judd*, in *Donald Judd* (cat.), Staatliche Kunsthalle Baden-Baden, 1989, p. 96.

32 Cf.: Donald Judd, *Nie wieder Krieg,* in *Kunst & Museumsjournaal*, no. 5, (1991), pp. 19–22; Donald Judd, *Imperialism, Nationalism and Regionalism (1975)*, in *Complete writings 1975–1986*, Stedelijk van Abbemuseum, Eindhoven 1987, pp. 125–136; Donald Judd, *(Statement),* in *The Artist and Politics. A Symposium*, in *Artforum* (Sept. 1970), p. 37.

33 Cf.: Donald Judd and Paul Taylor, *Interview with Donald Judd*, in *Flash Art* (May 1987), p. 37.

34 Ad Reinhardt, *25 Lines of Words on Art. Statement*, in Barbara Rose (ed.), *Art-as-Art. The Selected Writings of Ad Reinhardt*, New York 1975, p. 51.

35 Felix Gonzalez-Torres and Robert Storr, *Etre un espion* (interview), in *Art Press* (January 1995), p. 26.

36 Donald Judd, *(Statement)*, in *The Artist and Politics. A Symposium,* in *Artforum*, (Sept. 1970), p. 37.

37 Kurt Schwitters, *(Krieg ist die größte Schande) (1923)*, in Friedhelm Lach (ed.), *Das literarische Werk*, vol. 5, Cologne 1981, p. 146.

38 Donald Judd and Jochen Poetter, *Back to Clarity. Interview with Donald Judd*, in *Donald Judd* (cat.), Staatliche Kunsthalle Baden-Baden, 1989, p. 103.

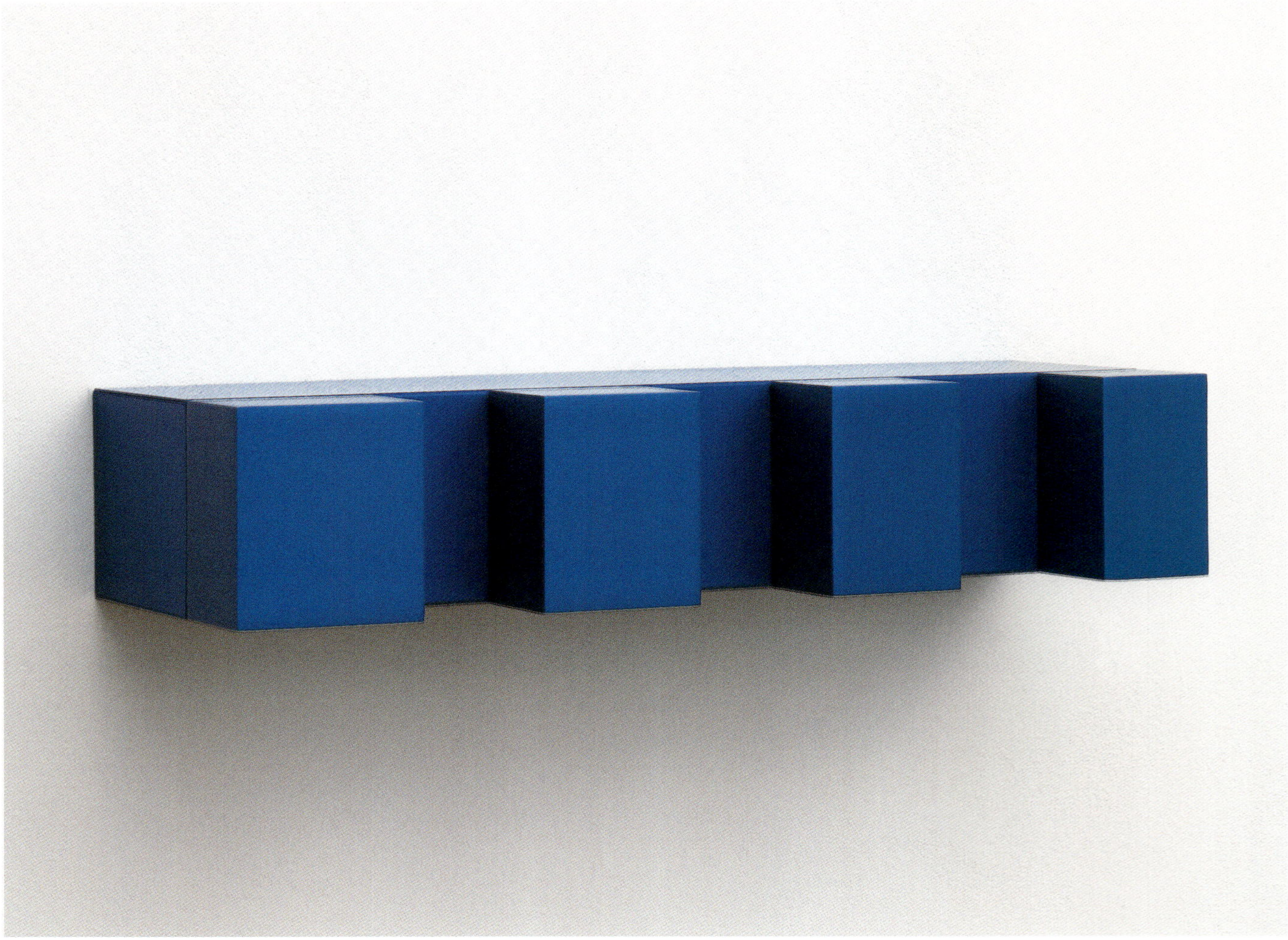

Untitled, 1988, anodized aluminum, 5" x 25" x 9"

Donald Judd and the Endless Possibilities of Color

William C. Agee

Donald Judd was one of the most influential artists of his generation, and the sweep and accomplishment of his work continue to be felt in contemporary art. His work has been well studied, but until recently little attention has been paid to his color, one of the most salient and powerful aspects of his art. Whether sensuous or glitzy, high-keyed or subtle, mono- or polychromatic, it was always there, an essential core of his work's structure and character. Whether physical and palpable, or dematerialized and elusive, it was an unmistakable presence, a defining element of his art. Judd spoke directly to its importance: "Material, space, and color are the main aspects of visual art" and "color, like material, is what art is made from,"[1] he said. He described color as a "phenomenon," as "the most powerful force,"[2] more powerful even than form. There was no "end to the possibilities" for color, he declared, concluding that "it is best to consider everything as color."[3] His words were manifest in his art, from start to finish, in forty years of work.

His color was literally inescapable, but it has taken a surprisingly long time for its full importance to be realized. Early on in his career it often took observers by surprise,[4] even prompting one critic in 1971 to describe Judd, memorably, as a "closet hedonist."[5] There are several reasons for this delayed reaction. First, Minimalist art was described in terms of reduction and absence, as cold and impersonal, all terms that excluded recognition of color as a factor to be taken into account. Yet as early as 1966, Rosalind Krauss noted the "sensuous and even voluptuous" color in Judd's work, as well as its multiple allusions and illusions.[6] In 1968, I pointed out the fundamental importance of color to his art.[7] However, the view of Minimalism as a simple art prevailed, and criticism largely missed the color. It took thirty years to change, but where we once saw reduction and absence in Judd's work, we now see complexity and richness, above all in his use of color.

There are other reasons as well. We have discounted color and we have viewed it as suspect. We do not trust it. We have never fully accepted or understood that the emergence of color as an autonomous expressive and structural language has been a large part of the history of modern art. Rather, we have thought of color as a decorative extra, a kind of aesthetic nicety, but without real substance or meaning. Venetian *colore* was not given the same weight as Florentine *disegno*. In our times the graphic planes of Cubism have been considered more complex and therefore as more profound than the art of Matisse, whom Judd thought was the best artist of the century before Pollock.[8] As Judd liked to say, however, complicated is not the same as complex.[9] The very word 'decorative' is dismissive, connoting an art of minor consequence. In this century, the issue of the decorative has been with us since 1908 when Matisse uttered his famous "armchair" remark, misunderstood and misinterpreted then and now. Since then, all color painters, including the late Monet, Pierre Bonnard, Mark Rothko, Hans Hofmann, Morris Louis, Kenneth Noland, and Sam Francis, as well as Judd himself, have suffered the critical epithet of 'decorative', in the pejorative sense. David Batchelor has described this attitude toward color as a "strange and deep kind of loathing," a fear of corruption through color that he calls "chromaphobia"[10] and traces back to the Greeks.

We have no common language with which to discuss color, for the existing terminology is either impossibly technical and obtuse, or hopelessly romantic and vague. We don't trust our emotions or our eyes, and thus, as Judd noted, color is something we hardly even see.[11] In addition, color means different things in different fields, and the scientist, the philosopher, and the artist all have their own vocabularies. For the artist, color is hard to contain and is even "slippery."[12] "Color is hard to learn," Judd said, "since it is hard to know what is useful. The particulars must be the artist's own."[13] With no common ground or understanding, and with little discussion, it is small wonder that we have been unprepared to engage an art of color.

The psychology of color and its specific effects on us constitute yet another field of reference. It was a field alien to Judd, who felt that assigning moods and attributes to colors, as Kandinsky and Marc did, was arbitrary and unreliable. It was not 'useful' for Judd, who valued thought as much as feeling, and who never could never understand why red should enrage a bull. There was nothing theoretical or idealist about color for him. He thought of color as physical, as real and substantial, a material in its own right, a concrete formal entity to be explored and employed as he did other materials. Color might have meaning, or it might not, but like other things in the world, it existed, and as he said famously, "things that exist exist, and everything is on their side."[14] Judd worked with color pragmatically, as he worked with form and space, testing, experimenting, learning as he went, thereby raising empiricism to a methodology, a full-blown working process. To understand Judd, one must digest the countless drawings and color notes he made, as well as the color samples he collected, searching for the precise qualities he sought. For

Judd, as for all color artists, color was the stuff of the world, of art and life. The artist engages it and works with it and out of it, but the results are never a given, and always come as something of a surprise. From this process, Judd made stunning works of art, remarkable for their confluence of clarity and sheer beauty. These qualities today are hardly understood or valued, one more reason why we have been slow to embrace art based on color. There is, nevertheless, a history of color and abstract art in America still to be written to include some of this century's best art, and in that history Judd will have to be accorded a special place.

Judd's knowledge of color and its history was long and deep, more so than even Judd specialists understood until late in his life when he wrote about it in detail. Its roots go back to his childhood. Always curious and inquisitive, he had an instinctive interest in art, and apparently he always had a special eye for color. He remembered that red and black appealed to him as a child in Nebraska; it was a pair of colors said to be a favorite of the Lakota Indians, and later had special significance for him.[15] He absorbed the colors of the Asian ceramics in the collection at the Nelson-Atkins Museum of Art while living in Kansas City. In 1947 he visited the Philadelphia Museum of Art and was taken by the vivid color, especially the red, in the renowned Rogier van der Weyden altarpiece, arguably the greatest painting in the United States. There he was also impressed by Mondrian's color, which he later described as one of the "wonders of the world."[16] While studying Art History at Columbia University in the 1950s, when Meyer Schapiro was teaching there, he certainly furthered his awareness of color. There Judd probably first heard color theory discussed; by the end of his life he was versed in the writings of Goethe, Chevreul, Johannes Itten, Adolf Hoelzel, and Josef Albers.

His real immersion in color, however, would have dated from art school. Judd began as a painter at the Art Students League in New York in the early 1950s, and even after turning to three dimensions, he always thought as one. It was the history of painting that interested him, not sculpture. In this, Judd was preceded by David Smith, who sought to eliminate all differences, except that of dimension, between painting and sculpture, thereby eliminating one of the last hierarchies of modern art. By so doing, Smith, and subsequently Judd, opened up three-dimensional art to a world as free and as filled with possibilities as that of the painter. Judd experimented with van der Weyden's colors in art school as well as with those of other masters, among them Gerard David, Giorgione, Titian, and El Greco, whose work he saw in books and museums. Indeed, he seems to have taken careful note of color practice in every period, from modern art all the way back to Attic vase painting, Mayan art, Romanesque painting, Cimabue and Giotto, and illuminated medieval manuscripts.[17]

Judd's first abstract paintings were based on hard-edged biomorphic forms rendered in muted grays, blacks, and blues. In two paintings of 1956, however, he introduced a large horizontal bar of yellow, a color he later reported was based on his experience of Mondrian.[18] In 1960–1961, largely as a result of his engagement with recent American art, Judd's work underwent a dramatic change. He sought to eliminate the part-by-part composition as well as the spatial illusionism that for him characterized older systems of painting. His ambition was to continue and to extend, in new and personal ways, the unity and the immediacy, as well as the order, scale, and clarity, he found in the art of Jackson Pollock, Barnett Newman, Mark Rothko, and Clyfford Still, qualities Judd believed were largely determined by the painters' use of color. How the large areas of strong color in Newman, Rothko, and Still impacted on Judd is easy to understand, but Pollock as a colorist is another matter. Color is an important aspect of Pollock's work, but it has been neglected in favor of the role of his drawing, once more a question of *disegno* over *colore*, and it has hardly been discussed. Judd, almost alone, grasped the importance of color to Pollock. Here we need to remember that for all colorists, Judd included, color means far more than the mere selection of hues. By necessity, it must include the amount, density, surface, texture, transparency, reflectivity, method of application, tone, value, proportion, scale, size, relation to and interaction with adjacent colors and materials. These are all complex and elusive matters, the very matters that make color so difficult to use effectively. Judd credited Pollock (and later, Albers as well) with the "most particular innovations" in color, including its "diversity, materiality, particularity and immediacy," and his use of color as a material. Judd noted that in Pollock: "The dripped paint is dripped paint, that sensation, complete, immediate, and unmotified ... it articulates the surface of the canvas."[19] Judd responded to Pollock's interest in a "specific and rigorous" surface in which the colors were more "discrete" than usual, with the areas seldom overlapping or ambiguous, and which maintained surface continuity and integrity, with no "holes or protuberances". He liked as well the large scale and fairly simple parts in Pollock and Newman. Judd understood that these artists were part of a tradition of color use that included Matisse, Léger, and Milton Avery.[20] He held Matisse in particular esteem, and admired his variety of hue, shape, and form, as well as his scale and a "lightness"[21] in his color that became particularly important to him. Judd admired Matisse's cutouts for their sheer size and scale, which were comparable to Pollock and Newman, as well as their materiality and brilliant hues.

Color came to real prominence in Judd's work in 1960–61. In a series of *line* paintings, he incised several lines, then a single curving one from top to bottom on a surface composed of a strong monochromatic mat color, a blue, a black, a red. It was as if Judd had isolated and clarified a single line from a Pollock drip

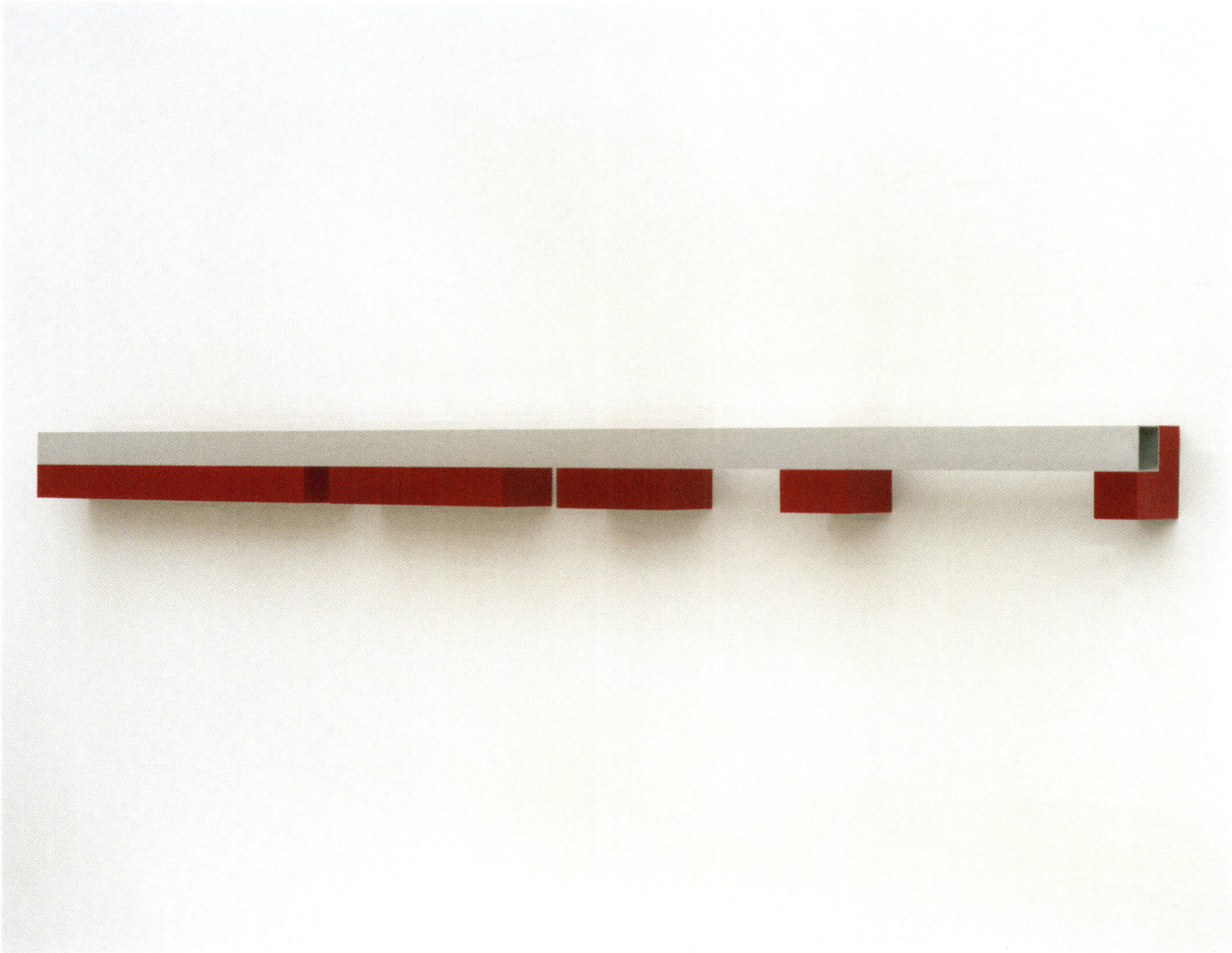

Untitled, 1969, lacquer on anodized aluminum, 6 1/8" x 110 3/4" x 6" (cat. no. 7)

painting or even a Newman *zip*, now curved, within large expanses of color that emulated the chromatic walls of Newman, Rothko, and Still with the clear and articulated surfaces he attributes to Pollock. By later 1961 Judd moved to an even greater immediacy by incorporating a geometric format of parallel horizontal lines located directly at the center. Color here became a truly material surface, made all the more so by a dense mat texture and, at times, the addition of sand. Color augmented, and even determined, the physical presence of the painting, creating the small, concrete order he was seeking.

By 1962, Judd had come to believe that he could go not further with Pollock, Newman, Rothko, and Still, for their achievement "could not be surpassed." This meant that "the century's development of color could continue no further on a flat surface ... Color to continue had to occur in space."[22] It was inevitable, for Judd had also come to believe that painting, by definition, no matter how reductive its format, was always going to contain a degree of illusionism. His solution was to move into three dimensions, first in reliefs (ill. pp. 10, 15) and then into freestanding pieces in 1962–1963 (ill. p. 18). In the reliefs, he could use red and black, a combination he placed special emphasis on, tracing its history back to Attic vase painting, the Lakota of his childhood, or to the codices of the Maya, for whom the colors represented wisdom.[23] For Judd, color did not carry meaning, or psychological implications, but it did certainly bring with it personal and historical associations. He had used the international blue of Yves Klein's monochrome paintings because he liked its non-illusionistic qualities. Now, however, he discontinued both it and black in favor of a strong, aggressive cadmium red, both light and medium, which became a signature color in his early work. He favored it because its lighter, more precise feel defined the edges of the forms more exactly than the darker hues. The color now was coextensive with the surface of the painting, the color was the form and the material. "Color and space occur together,"[24] Judd noted.

While Judd had looked carefully at the work of earlier generations, he was also well aware of color of the younger artists who were his peers. His use of color paralleled the concurrent development of colorfield painting, notably in the work of Morris Louis, Kenneth Noland, and Frank Stella. Further, compositional methods were related. We can usefully compare the centering circle in Judd's 1962 relief (ill. p. 10) with Noland's concentric circle paintings of 1958–1963, or a four-part division of the red and black relief with the divisions in such black-stripe paintings of 1959 as the painting *Die Fahne Hoch!* by Frank Stella from the collection of the Whitney Museum of American Art in New York. John Chamberlain, a major American artist, is not generally thought of in terms of color, but he was important to Judd in this and other respects. In 1962 Judd termed Chamberlain "the only sculptor really using color, the full range ... his color is as particular, complex and structural as any painter's."[25] Both Chamberlain's applied paint and the color inherent in his crumpled automobile parts – "hard, sweet pastels" or dark, intense hues – struck Judd as instructive examples of ways in which color could articulate volume. Judd reacted with particular enthusiasm to the distinctive surface created by the chromatic luster of the Harley-Davidson metallic automotive lacquers (ill. p. xx) that Chamberlain had used in a little known series of geometric reliefs of 1964. Judd also took special notice of Stuart Davis, who, although not of his generation, was a distinctive colorist in his own right. In a review of what was to prove to be Davis' last one man show in 1962, Judd almost single-handedly rescued Davis from critical oblivion. "There should be applause,"[26] Judd wrote, in open admiration of the power, clarity and scale of Davis' work of the 60s, praising Davis' color as 'hot', as well as subtle and complex. Judd also pointed out Davis' theory of a color-space continuum, meaning that an area of color created and was synonymous with an equal area of space, a proposition that closely paralleled Judd's equation of color with space. He also admired Davis' insistence on clarity in art and thought, later quoting Davis' statement of 1940: "Confusion is simply confusion and clarity is fundamental to art."[27]

Judd's first three-dimensional pieces of 1963, such as the early low-lying boxes, were made of wood, painted cadmium red light (ill. p. 18). Wood, however, was limiting, for it was too absorbent, too much like canvas, lacking in the precision he was seeking. In coming years, he explored a wide range of industrial, non-art materials such as plexiglass, hot and cold rolled steel, aluminum, anodized aluminum, brushed aluminum, galvanized iron, brass, and stainless steel. Each had its own particular quality, including its own inherent color. Judd preferred, when possible, a natural hue that literally fused color and material in a single unity. Thus, one color was identical with one surface, always a tenet in his art, to avoid arbitrary divisions of a surface. As he expanded his range of materials, he simultaneously expanded his range of color. This fusion paralleled the manner in which paint soaked into the very fabric of colorfield canvases. It also calls to mind Brancusi and the surface colors and effects he distilled from various types of marble, and from bronze and brass. New materials, in particular, opened up fresh possibilities for Judd by enabling him to move to a greater variety of progressively lighter, more open, linear, and tensile formats. They defined volume, rather than density and mass, emblems of an older art and culture. In the plexiglass boxes (ill. p. 28) and stacks (ill. pp. 107–109), for example, we peer into that volume, making the work seem much lighter than it actually is. At all costs, Judd avoided the appearance of weight.

By 1968, Judd had forged a vibrant range of color, rivaled only by Chamberlain and Dan Flavin, that included red, orange, amber, green, and dark brown plexiglass; automotive paints, such

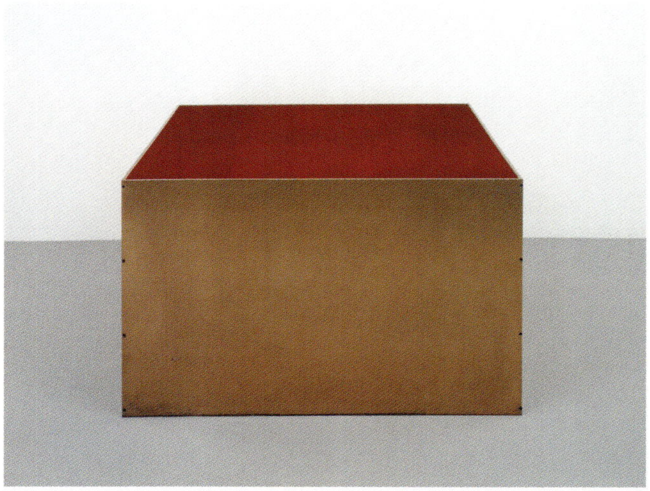

Untitled, 1972, copper, enameled aluminum, 36" x 60" x 36"

as Harley-Davidson Hi-Fi red, blue, and purple, and 1958 Chevrolet Regal Turquoise baked into the surface; and the natural color and reflections of brass, steel, and aluminum. Variations of inherent color could turn the same format into clearly separate and distinct pieces, as in the same progressions, one made of reflective brass and the other of dull galvanized iron (ill. p. 25). In turn, the combination of two materials each with its own color offered variant combinations, as in the plexiglass box with the steel ends. Or an applied color could be contrasted with a natural one, such as in the 1969 progression from the collection of the Louisiana Museum of Modern Art in Humlebaek, combining red painted with clear anodized aluminum (ill. p. 37). As he worked with materials, so he worked with color; one could not be separated from the other. For example, by using transparent, translucent, or opaque plexiglass, Judd could vary both the color and the volume of the piece. In turn, other changes were effected by the various combinations of materials in the stacks: first, there was solid material, then plexiglass on top and bottom with metal sides, and then, finally, wraparound plexiglass. Judd disliked the primary colors and their predictable harmonies. He favored unusual, and unexpected hues, and he found them by searching for commercial and industrial paints, as he had searched for new industrial materials. As David Batchelor has pointed out, the works were assembled and arranged in industrial fashion, rather than manipulated in the studio: with the color, they were "built rather than crafted, whole rather than

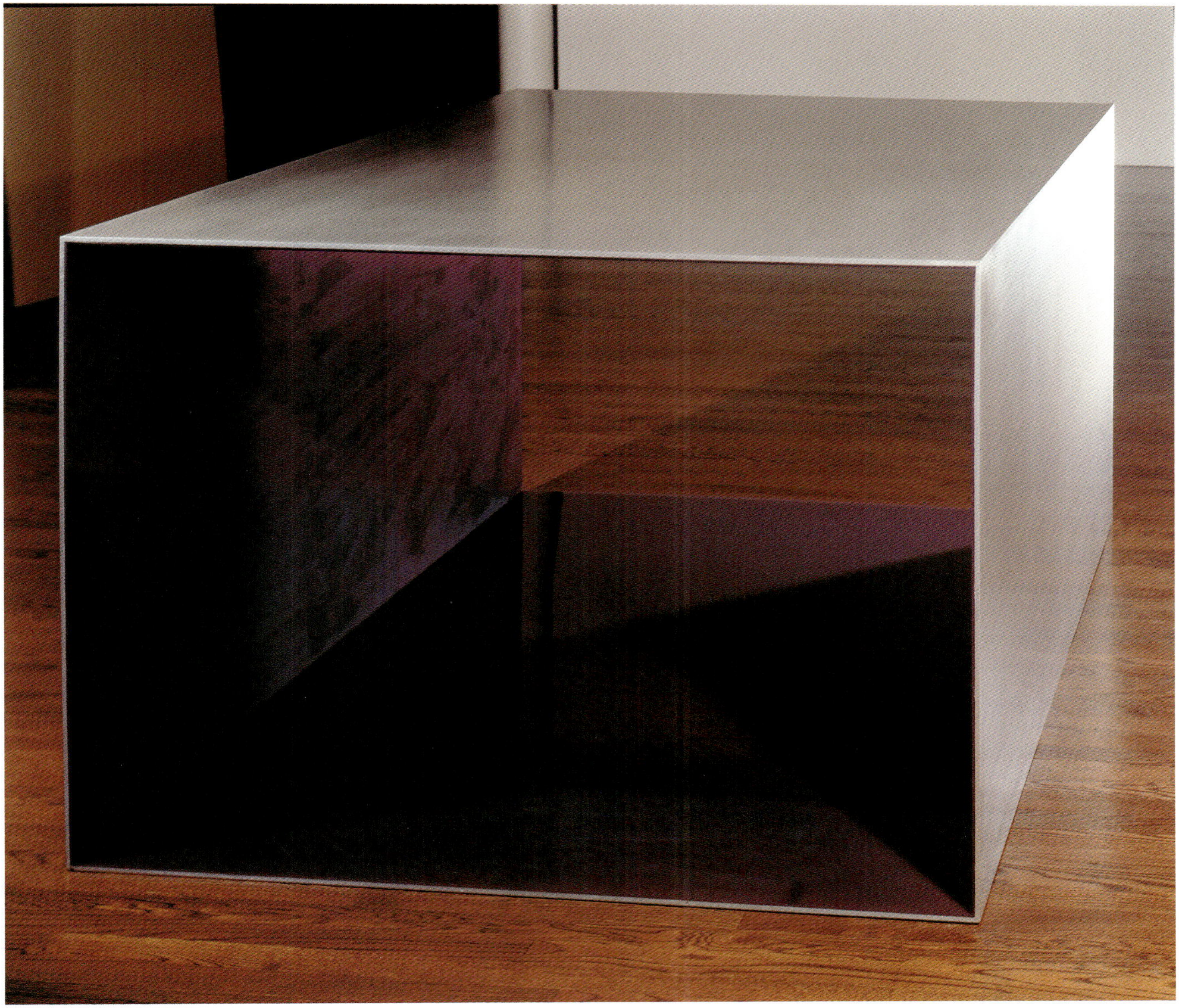

Untitled, 1969, clear anodized aluminum, plexiglass, 33" x 68" x 48" (cat. no. 6)

pictorial, planar rather than solid, synthetic rather than organic, regular rather than irregular; these characteristics are also the characteristics of our modernity."[28]

These colors and materials transformed what were perceived as clear and simple in much contemporary discussion of Minimalism into ever-shifting objects of multiple complexities and references. They went largely unnoticed except by Rosalind Krauss who pointed out the "extraordinary beauty and authority"[29] of Judd's work, noting the use of violet and brushed aluminum in the twenty-foot span of a progression, as well as its irrational perspective. In retrospect, we can now see that elements of ambiguity informed Judd's work from the start. Even in his first box of 1963, the nature of the space within the progression cut into the top, for example, eludes us. Had we been more observant at the time, we might also have noticed the several kinds of illusion created by the reflections of the multiple colors of plexiglass and solid materials Judd used in his boxes and stacks of 1965–1971. Depending on the light, plexiglass will fluoresce and appear to change into another color altogether, thus confounding the very identity of a specific piece, a phenomenon which can be verified by cataloguers of Judd's work. Further, we receive varying degrees of information on the nature of the interior volumes depending on the relative transparency of a given color of plexiglass. Solid and void are also confounded in the brass box of 1969 because the top is lowered, and the resulting shadows and reflections virtually dissolve our sense of the work as a single, discrete entity.

The stacks can be especially perplexing. In the 1994 stack with purple plexiglass (ill. p. 109) on the sides and copper on the tops and bottoms, solid and void are apparently reversed because the darkness of the plexiglass appears as solid and the highly reflective copper as open. Colors change in relation to each other, both as solid and void, and change yet again as they reflect on the wall (ill. p. 108). Color, then, not only defines volume, it becomes volume itself. We can now see these works for what they were, an intense, systematic investigation of color and materials within a given format, although at the time, they were often found repetitious and decorative. As Judd cut into material (or directed his fabricator to cut) he worked as Matisse had with his cutouts, for when he cut directly into the material he simultaneously cut into his color. The quality of the materials – thick or thin, soft or hard, pliable or resistant, shiny or dull – became the qualities of his color as well.

That Judd's art was informed as much as by "sensual mystery"[30] as by analytic clarity became inescapably apparent by 1975. In a series of open brass boxes begun in 1972 (ill. p. 40), the bottom was painted red, causing reflections of red on the sides of the box. These reflections vary in shape, substance, and extent, depending on our viewing position. They alter our perceptions as we approach, and even fool us into thinking that the sides are at least partially painted. It is only after peering into the box that we understand the source of the color and the nature of its effects.[31] The experience is something like that of the dispersed light in a room with work by Flavin, but now contained in one piece. The piece tells us, once more, that it is only by our own immediate visual experience that we can grasp material reality.

It is as if Judd's drive to the lightness of color he had always preferred had led him to the literal use of real light. Judd never spoke much about light and its effects, but it is an essential aspect of his color. Such effects grew incrementally in his work and were taken to another level altogether in the installation of one hundred milled aluminum pieces in the two Artillery sheds at his compound in Marfa, Texas, completed by 1984 (ill. p. 45). Each piece opens and defines a different spatial configuration according to multiple divisions within the basic rectangular box. As the strong light of West Texas streams in and over these works, the interplay of multiple, shifting planes and perspectives of silver light creates a literally dazzling experience, rightly suggesting that the use of light here recalls Mark Rothko in its creations of weightless, illusory surfaces.[32] The fragmentation and even dematerialization of planes is complete; solids and voids become interchangeable as in a Cubist painting by Davis. We can hardly distinguish between the material and the immaterial; light, both natural and reflected, transforms the works into a state of flux that moves beyond our ability to comprehend it. It was as if Judd had responded to the California light artists, Larry Bell and Robert Irwin, both of whom he admired, now with a largeness of vision seldom in modern art. Light and color are the unifying forces, creating an almost perfect union of art, architecture, and site, conceived and carried out in total harmony with the expanse of the West Texas landscape and sky. The installation is an inspiring integration of the arts, recalling the ideals of William Morris, Albers and the Bauhaus, and Mondrian, van Doesburg and De Stijl artists, but on a vast and previously inconceivable scale. Judd insisted his art avoided large systems, but his practice suggests otherwise. Finally, he might have concurred. Judd was fond of telling two stories about this installation. His friend, the poet and writer Hannah Green remarked that the installation was "almost sublime," to which Judd responded, "why almost?" Then, too, after touring the installation a Jesuit priest told Judd that they were both in the same business.[33]

The illusionism of these pieces continued – and expanded – in the late 1980s in a series of open aluminum floor boxes (ill. pp. 94, 95) with interior sections of blue anodized aluminum, divided by both blue plexiglass and aluminum panels. Another in this series was divided by a black anodized aluminum panel, where earlier Judd had shunned the use of black (ill. pp. 96, 97). Our sense of uncertainty and ambiguity as to the source of color and its now multiple reflections looked back to the red painted brass boxes of 1972–1975 (ill. p. 40), but the complexity and

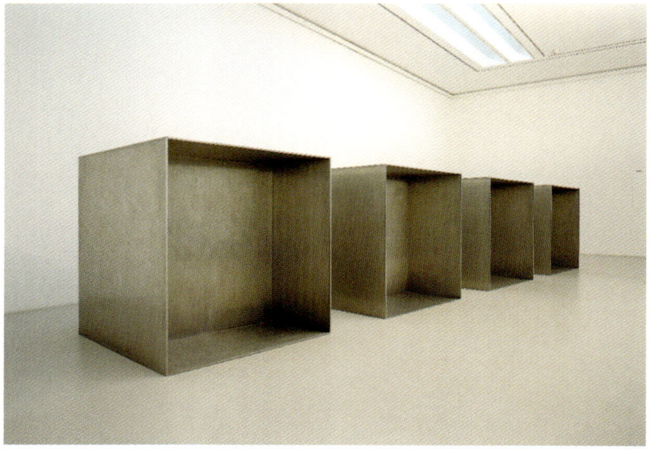

Untitled, 1977, iron, nickel, 4 units, each 59" x 59" x 59"

permutations of color and light had increased exponentially. What is material and what is illusion is called into question at every turn. The possibilities were indeed endless. Color changed according to the nature of the material from which it emanated, and changed once more when reflected onto another type of surface. We need also remember that these changes were in turn subjected to the permutations of hue, value, and tone, thus tripling the transformations rendered by color. In a sense, Judd's art had come full circle, for where he had renounced illusionism and certain effects in his paintings, he now embraced and elaborated on them at every turn. It is the essence of Judd, who "confounds so many assumptions,"[34] to come back to an earlier idea and transform it in light of his current concerns, much as Stuart Davis had done.

In the 1970s and early 1980s, Judd concurrently explored other modes of color and visual complexity. These relied not on the luster of aluminum and plexiglass, but on the understated surfaces of plywood, a material he had also once rejected. Its plainness enabled him to work on an unprecedented scale in a piece of 1981 that extended a full 11 by 77 feet. For all its plainness, however, the sheer amount of the material, its broad sweep, and the moiré patterns of the surface endow this piece with a tactile richness, another kind of the hue that makes us understand Judd's dictum that everything should be understood as color. There are three systems of division and articulation, giving the work a "controlled, complex unity"[35] that suggests nothing less than Pollock's mural-sized paintings. The multiple divisions also recall the increased number of lines that Mondrian introduced

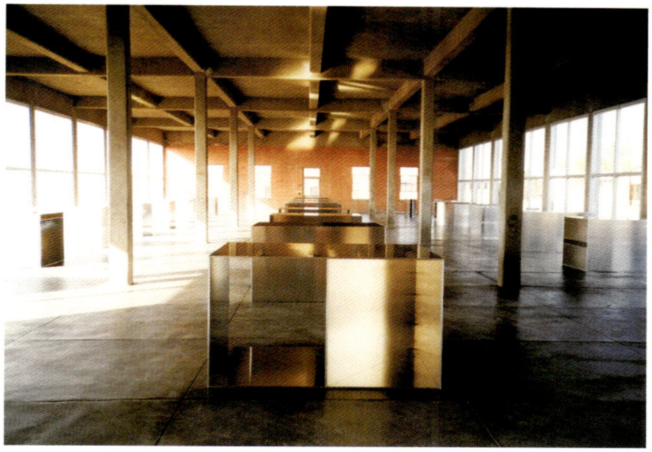

The Chinati Foundation, Marfa, north artillery shed with permanent installation of 52 works

into his paintings of 1938–1942. In each case there was a drive to increasing complexity that Judd paralleled.

The parallel was not accidental. Judd, we need to remember, always thought as a painter. As his powers and his assurance grew, as he understood that he could work on their level, Judd openly engaged the masters of modern art. Foremost among them was Mondrian. Judd had always admired his color ("a wonder of the world"), but he had separated himself in the 1960s from Mondrian's compositional methods of part-by-part relational balancing. Moving beyond this earlier stance, he came to believe that Mondrian was, without reservation, one of the greatest artists of the twentieth century. He deeply admired Mondrian's clarity, probity, and particularly his inventiveness, which he emulated in his own drive to greater complexity. Further, in Mondrian's goal of unifying the arts to make a better society, Judd found a lifelong purpose, the animating ideal behind his installations in Texas.[36] As his knowledge of it increased, he also came to respect the work of Malevich, for what he termed his "independent form and color,"[37] and his nonillusionistic space. Most especially, Judd championed the work of Albers, an artist whom he had underestimated at first but later came to hold in the highest regard.[38] He admired the meticulous investigation of color that Albers had undertaken over a lifetime. Albers' influential book *Interaction of Color* (1963), particularly its emphasis on color as material, was well known to him. Also important to Judd was the way in which Albers integrated color and composition, with color and surface fusing as a material. All three of these artists had been pivotal in extending art into daily life, a practice Judd himself furthered by his work in architecture and design, realms in which color also played an important role.

That Judd's methods, indeed, his instincts, revolved around painting was demonstrated by his continuing use of the wall. The stacks and progressions were always associated with the wall, of course, but they were aggressively three-dimensional, projecting away from the wall as if to distance themselves from painting. In 1974, however, Judd began a series of self-framing, open horizontal wall boxes lined at the back with plexiglass that because of their openness, discrete size, and insistent frontality seemed once more to engage painting overtly (ill. pp. 85–89). We look at these works as we look at paintings, head on, reading the flat surface of the plexiglass at back as identified with the wall, the framing edges now projecting into real space. For Judd, the challenge was to maintain the integrity of a flat surface on a flat wall, but to do it in a form other than of a two-dimensional painting.

The first of this series consisted of a stainless steel 'frame' backed by blue plexiglass over cadmium red plexiglass, creating a dark admixture against the shining steel, the reflections reverberating inside the box much the same way they did in the brass floor boxes. In subsequent works in this format, he combined either anodized aluminum, Cor-ten steel, or stainless steel in the frame with an astonishing range of colored plexiglass at the back. As always, the same plexiglass used with different materials produced significantly altered effects; red combined with the deep rich rust color of Cor-ten was very different from it appearance when combined with the soft grays of aluminum or with the highly reflective surfaces of stainless steel. Even greater complexity was achieved when Judd added one, two, or three divisions to the boxes, either of plain material, anodized aluminum, or colored plexiglass. He could use red and black, a combination of colors that was an old favorite (ill. p. 87), or blue by itself (ill. p. 85), but no matter how many surfaces he introduced, each retained a single color. In 1992, in a particularly remarkable work, he incorporated a range of novel hues including green, yellow, purple, ivory, orange, and black plexiglass, each used separately, in six Cor-ten boxes aligned vertically (ill. p. 113). The multiplicity of effects was extended in other ways when he incorporated color into the aluminum, as in the black anodized aluminum box with the turquoise anodized divider. More perceptual shifts followed when he oriented the divider horizontally, at varying depths within the box, to contrast and echo the blue over red plexiglass at the back (ill. p. 86).

In all cases, however, we read these works serially, as panel paintings of color, divided sequentially, as Mondrian divided his paintings, now made three-dimensional. By the end of Judd's life, so deep was his admiration for Albers that he credited Albers, along with Pollock for the "most particular" innovations in color. They were the same qualities as those of Pollock, the materiality, diversity, immediacy, particularity, the color as material, and in Albers, the way a color actually changed throughout an area. These were the very qualities that had come to distinguish Judd's color. That Judd went to a square format in 1993, using yellow plexiglass at the back of a plywood box, seemed to be an obvious acknowledgement of Albers' *Hommage to the Square* series, combined with a reference to the 'zips' of Barnett Newman in the wooden columns dividing the pieces. There was much else in Albers' use of color that interested Judd: the identity of color varied according to the expanse of the areas; the color varied according to the colors surrounding it and thus also has an identity as a changed color; the painting was a single whole and was "as complex as a metope;"[39] the scheme of squares and the corresponding change of color provided changes in proportion, an idea of special interest to Judd.

Despite his explorations, however, Judd still felt constricted, for he had not found a way to work with more than two or three colors at once. By 1983, like an impatient painter, his appetite for color was insatiable. He wanted to use "more and diverse bright colors than before,"[40] all of them, all at once, with a multiplicity that even he had not previously known. Working back and forth, as he liked to do, he shifted from the understatement of the large plywood piece of 1981 to a barrage of full colors seen simultaneously. In effect, he wished to translate the linear complexity of the plywood into a parallel complexity generated by color alone. His solution was ingenious: he created what amount to volumes of pure color by bolting together recessed sections of varying lengths of painted sheet aluminum (ill. pp. 52–75). In these he could work like a true painter, opening color up in ways not previously possible.

The first two of these works were large, freestanding floor pieces which established the underlying principle of joining separate sections of multiple colors on all sides and on top, so that we see nothing but color (ill. p. 52). Judd soon moved the pieces to the wall, where the permutations of format could be expanded and where even the bottom of the piece can be experienced as pure color (ill. pp. 60, 61). The color had to be applied because it was the only way in which Judd could get the variety he wanted, but so total is the fusion of color and material that we perceive only color. These pieces are the ultimate fusion of painting and three dimensions, for they are formed with what amount to bars of distinct color, traceable to the yellow bars that Judd extrapolated from Mondrian in his first abstract paintings of 1956. Their colored multiforms recall the dense, optical patterning of Mondrian's last paintings, *Broadway Boogie Woogie* and *Victory Boogie Woogie*, of 1942–1943. At the same time, the multiple patterns of color in the work of Al Jensen, and that of Richard Paul Lohse and Olle Baertling,[41] all well known to Judd, also bear comparison to these works, as does Albers' mural in the PanAm building, as it was then named.

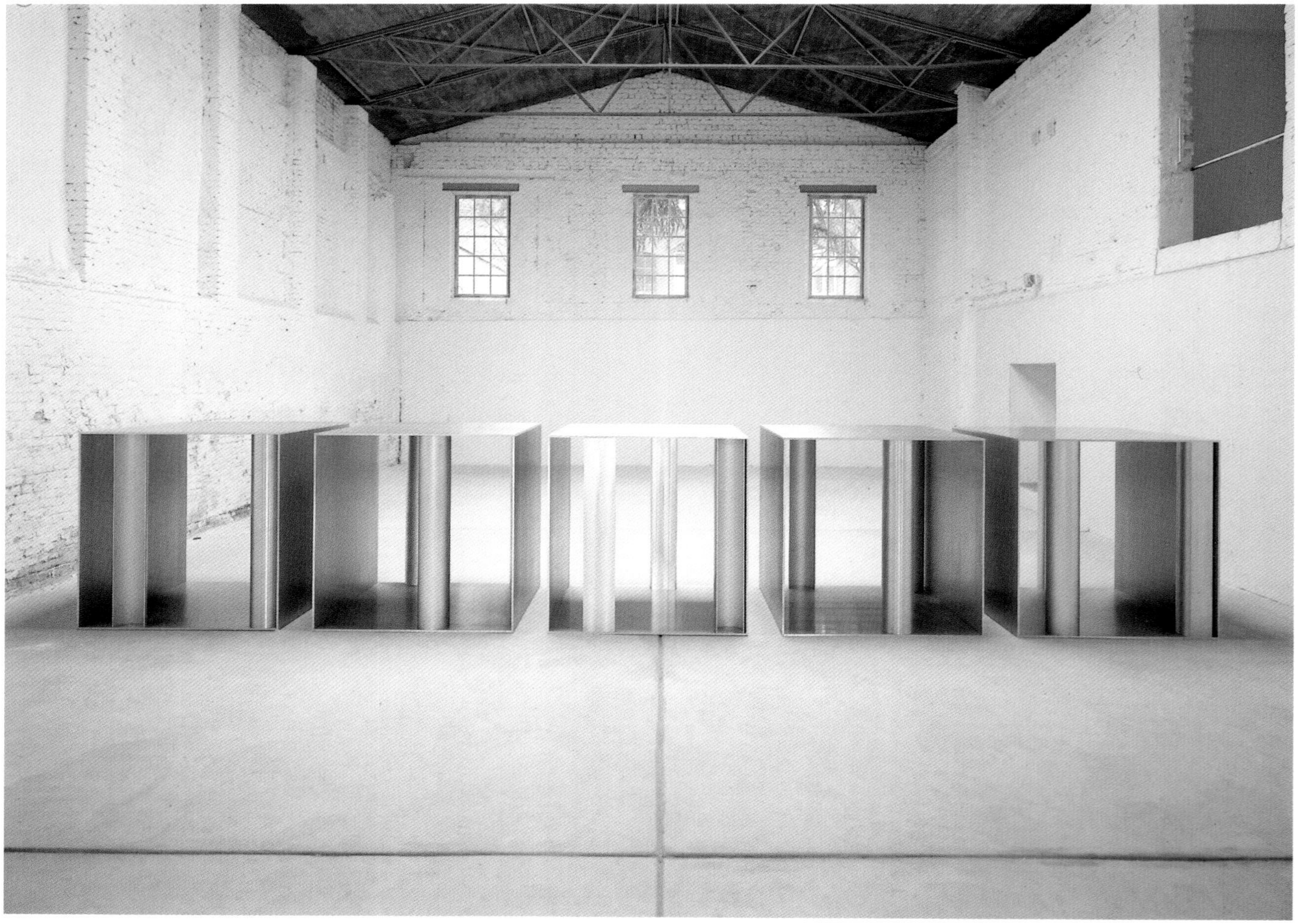

Untitled, 1991, aluminum, 5 units, each 59" x 59" x 59"

Judd did not want the colors to combine, especially in ways that characterized his older work; nor did he want the colors to form easy harmonies or deliberate disharmonies. Further, he did not want the same color ever to be immediately contiguous. Each color had to be clear and distinct, particular, independent, as in Malevich. Judd was looking for something new and original, as he always had. He set limits, as Albers had done with concentric squares. The limitations were radical; the solution to them was not easy. He had to rethink color and its usage: how much color, in what combinations and how one color affects and inflects another. It was made all the more difficult because his colors were intense, taken from the RAL standard industrial color chart, and made in Europe where Judd felt color was purer than in the United States. Judd did not want easy harmonies, but certainly did not want chaos either, and bright colors, he felt, could easily destroy the unity of a piece.

The construction therefore required careful planning and testing, demanding far more than the immediacy of the bright colors would suggest. Judd used schemes and sequences, but they are usually not obvious, and in some cases they are not yet apparent, telling us that, like the progressions, they are not rigid. The matter is complicated by the fact that the colors are arranged to read both horizontally, vertically, and diagonally, as well in relation to the other three sides; some are two-piece works (ill. pp. 63, 65), one over the other, one echoing the other in dual responses. They could be small or large, with the amounts and proportions of color varying in each, a matter of utmost importance to Judd. They could be a simple arrangement of two colors, as in the red and black piece (ill. p. 72), once more his favorite pair, used in spite of himself. They were generally far more complicated, however, even using all possible combinations of either four or eight colors in a given work. Judd made notes of schemes as varied as (A+B) or (B+C) or (A+B) + (B+C) + (C+D) and so on.[42] Other schemes are evident, among them (A+B+A) and (A+B+C+A). They involved the use of pairs and triads, well known in color theory. Judd believed that some pairs, such as red and black, were so familiar that they become one color, a two-color monochrome. Every color paired with black and white became a monochrome. For Judd, all colors of the same value made pairs, and all values of the same color made pairs. Then there were pairs opposed, such as cobalt blue and cerulean blue, or cobalt blue and cadmium red light.[43] The same sequence of monochromes and contrasting colors applied to triads as well: red, black, and white were monochromatic, for example. Much of this had to do with longstanding principles of color usage, referring back to Chevreul, Seurat and modern abstract painting, such as the law of harmony of contrast, the law of simultaneous contrast, and the gradation of hue and value. But above all, no matter which sequence was used, there would be, finally, "only color."[44] In these works, Judd's color became something more, beyond painting or sculpture. It became a virtually new and independent medium, as Matisse's cutouts were, all fulfilling an old prophecy of modern art, championed by the American critic Willard Huntington Wright and others.[45]

In Judd's hands, color became at once surface, volume, space, material, the organizing and unifying principle, and the very essence of his work. Judd liked to say that there was far more variety to his art than was casually apparent, and this is true, due in large part to the variety of his color. Indeed, everything was color for Judd, even the rich adobe and stone walls he built in Marfa and at his ranch at Ayala de Chinati, a pronounced contrast to the vivid color of the baked-enamel sheet aluminum pieces. Judd had extended his involvement with the wall and painting to a consideration of the wall as an independent architectural element in which color became a literal, tactile texture, another facet of color. Judd's wall was part of an integration of art, architecture, and all the arts, "to improve the quality of the civilization." Color is an essential part of that integration and of the natural world, recalling Matisse's painting *Joie de Vivre* at the Barnes Foundation, Merion, PA. In color there is the variety and the vitality of the world, part of "the existence of everything and the space and time that is created by existing things", as he said. Art is made as one lives, he insisted, and Judd pursued color and its endless possibilities as he pursued life itself, "all the way out."[46]

Notes

1 Donald Judd, *Some aspects of color in general and red and black in particular*, (Speech held on the occasion of the award ceremony for the Sikkens Foundation Prize, on 27 November 1993 in the Stedelijk Museum Amsterdam), Sikkens Foundation, Sassenheim/Stedelijk Museum Amsterdam, 1993. In this volume: pp. 79–116. Other information not cited herein comes from conversations between Judd and the author held over many years beginning in 1966.

2 Donald Judd, *Some aspects of color in general and red and black in particular (1993)*, in this volume: pp. 79, 98, 114.

3 Donald Judd and Jochen Poetter, *Back to Clarity. Interview with Donald Judd* (interview), in *Donald Judd* (cat.), Staatliche Kunsthalle Baden-Baden, 1989, pp. 87, 94.

4 Cf. James Mellow, *Everything Sculpture Has, My Work Doesn't*, in: *The New York Times*, 10 March 1968, pp. 21, 26.

5 Hilton Kramer, *Display of Judd Art Defines an Attitude*, in *The New York Times*, 14 May 1971, p. 48.

6 Rosalind Krauss, *Allusion and Illusion in Donald Judd*, in *Artforum*, May 1966, pp. 24–26.

7 Cf. William C. Agee, *Don Judd,* in *Donald Judd* (cat.), Whitney Museum of American Art, New York 1968, unpaginated.

8 Donald Judd, *Statement on Matisse*, in *Art in America*, July/Aug. 1975, p. 71.

9 Donald Judd to Marianne Stockebrand, now Director of the Chinati Foundation, and his long-time companion.

10 David Batchelor, *Chromaphobia, Ancient and Modern, and a Few Notable Exceptions*, in *Art & Design*, July/Aug. 1997, pp. 31/32.

11 Cf. Donald Judd, *Some aspects of color in general and red and black in particular (1993)*, in this volume p. 79.

12 David Batchelor, *Chromaphobia, Ancient and Modern, and a Few Notable Exceptions*, in *Art & Design*, July/Aug. 1997, p. 32.

13 Donald Judd, *Some aspects of color in general and red and black in particular (1993)*, in this volume p. 92.

14 Donald Judd, *Black, White, and Gray (1964)*, in *Complete Writings 1959–1975*, Halifax/New York 1975, p. 117.

15 This and the following information was described in Donald Judd, *Some aspects of color in general and red and black in particular (1993)*, in this volume esp. p. 116.

16 Donald Judd, *Some aspects of color in general and red and black in particular (1993)*, in this volume p. 98.

17 Cf. Donald Judd, *Some aspects of color in general and red and black in particular (1993)*, in this volume pp. 81–82.

18 Reported by Marianne Stockebrand to the author.

19 Donald Judd, *Abstract Expressionism (1983)*, in *Complete Writings 1975–1986*, Stedelijk van Abbemuseum, Eindhoven 1987, pp. 44–47.

20 Cf. Donald Judd, *Abstract Expressionism (1983),* in *Complete Writings 1975–1986*, Stedelijk van Abbemuseum, Eindhoven 1987, pp. 44–47.

21 Donald Judd and David Batchelor, *A Small Kind of Order: Donald Judd* (interview), in *Artscribe International,* Nov./Dec. 1989, p. 64

22 Donald Judd, *Some aspects of color in general and red and black in particular (1993)*, in this volume p. 112.

23 Cf. Donald Judd, *Some aspects of color in general and red and black in particular (1993)*, in this volume p. 116.

24 Donald Judd, *Some aspects of color in general and red and black in particular (1993)*, in this volume p. 110.

25 Donald Judd, *John Chamberlain (1962)*, in *John Chamberlain. New Sculpture* (cat.), The Pace Gallery, New York 1989, p. II. All of Judd's writings on Chamberlain were reprinted in this catalogue.

26 Donald Judd, *Stuart Davis (1962)*, in *Complete Writings 1959–1975*, Halifax/New York 1975, pp. 55/56.

27 Donald Judd and Jochen Poetter, *Back to Clarity. Interview with Donald Judd* (interview), in *Donald Judd* (cat.), Staatliche Kunsthalle Baden-Baden, 1989, p. 87.

28 David Batchelor, *Chromaphobia, Ancient and Modern, and a Few Notable Exceptions*, in *Art & Design*, July/Aug. 1997, pp. 32/33.

29 Rosalind Krauss, *Allusion and Illusion in Donald Judd*, in: *Artforum*, May 1966, p. 24.

30 Thomas McEvilley, *Donald Judd*, in *Artforum*, February 1989, p. 125.

31 These effects were first described in: William C. Agee, *Unit, Series, Site: A Judd Lexicon*, in *Art in America*, May/June 1975, pp. 40–49.

32 Cf. Carol Rosen, *Donald Judd at Marfa*, in *Arts Magazine*, Sept. 1988, p. 40.

33 For a fuller discussion see: William C. Agee, *Donald Judd in Retrospect: An Appreciation*, in *Donald Judd. Sculpture* (cat.), The Pace Gallery, New York 1994, pp. 14–15.

34 Jed Perl, *After Judd: Notes at season's end*, in *The New Criterion*, June 1994, p. 38.

35 Cf. Roberta Smith, *Multiple Returns*, in *Art in America*, March 1982, pp. 112–114.

36 Cf. Donald Judd, *Art and Architecture (1983)*, in *Complete Writings 1975–1986*, Stedelijk van Abbemuseum, Eindhoven 1987, pp. 25–36.

37 Donald Judd, *Malevich: Independent Form, Color, Surface (1974)*, in *Complete Writings 1959–1975*, Halifax/New York 1975, pp. 211–215.

38 Cf. Donald Judd, *Josef Albers*, in *Josef Albers* (cat.), The Chinati Foundation, Marfa 1991, pp. 14–25.

39 Donald Judd, *Josef Albers*, in: *Josef Albers* (cat.), The Chinati Foundation, Marfa 1991, p. 24.

40 Donald Judd, *Some aspects of color in general and red and black in particular (1993)*, in this volume p. 114.

41 Cf. *Donald Judd, Some aspects of color in general and red and black in particular (1993)*, in this volume p. 116.

42 Cf. Donald Judd, *Some aspects of color in general and red and black in particular (1993)*, in this volume p. 115.

43 Cf. Donald Judd, *Some aspects of color in general and red and black in particular (1993)*, in this volume p. 115.

44 Donald Judd, *Some aspects of color in general and red and black in particular (1993)*, in this volume p. 115.

45 See, for example, Willard Huntington Wright, *The Future of Painting*, New York 1923.

46 All quotes in this paragraph are from Donald Judd, *Art and Architecture* (1983), in *Complete writings 1975–1986*, Stedelijk van Abbemuseum, Eindhoven 1987, p. 32.

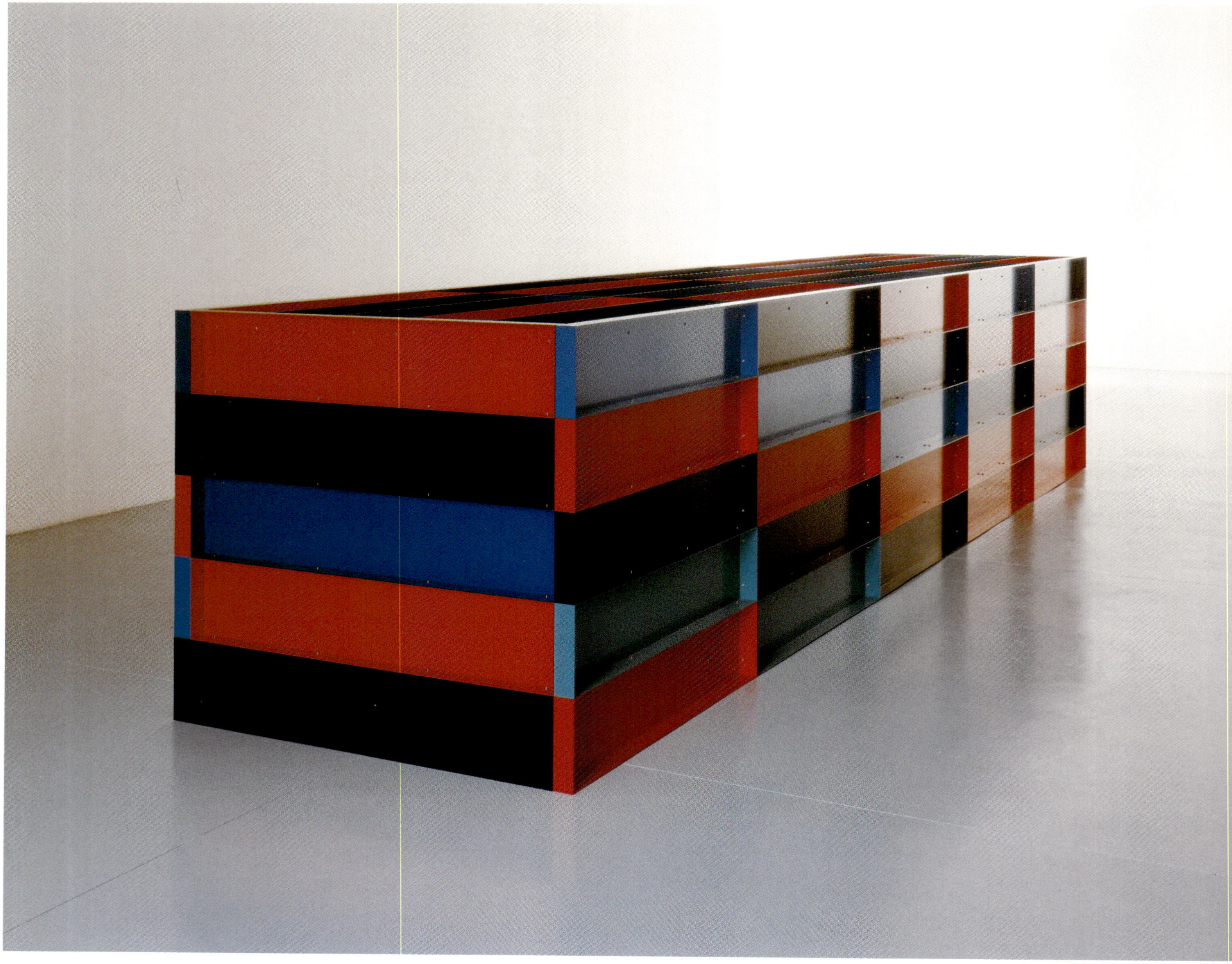

Untitled, 1984, enameled aluminum, 59" x 65" x 295"

Specific Objects – The Illusion of Factuality

Martin Engler

"Were Judd's works to be as limited as his pronouncements have suggested, it would fail." Elisabeth Baker

Everything could really be so simple: Flavin's fluorescent tubing, Andre's cobble-stones, Morris' fiber glass objects and Judd's metal boxes – industrially produced materials and a stereometric formal vocabulary, all ordered non-hierarchically, somehow without reference, and immediately understandable as a whole. Up to this very day, Minimal Art continues to be defined by reference to a basically ambiguous title and a handy canon of its formal means, which, as the 'lowest common denominator', provides only a very inadequate and sketchy description of its qualities and, above all, of the individual positions of its main representatives. This soberly stringent definition of Minimal Art says little about the peculiarities of the various positions, or about what constitutes its undisputed and essential contribution to twentieth century art. In the following, I aim to highlight the productive and instructive tension which is created, particularly in the case of Judd, between the stringent rhetoric of Minimal Art and the undeniably sensual qualities of its works, between the stringent rhetoric of Minimal art and its multifarious perception.[1] Taking a new look at the simultaneity of apparently irreconcilable aspects could uncover a central building block in the still imprecisely defined theory of Minimal Art. The label Minimal Art, though practically robbed of all meaning due to its inflationary and unspecific use in recent years, could thus undergo a wide-ranging re-definition as far as Judd is concerned, indeed perhaps not just Judd.

If one abandons for a moment the comfortable security of the stringent Minimal raster, then alongside the Donald Judd of the non-referential industrial product and the stereometric series one finds a Minimalist Judd, whose formal vocabulary subverts the supposed clarity of the forms and whose varied and sensual range of materials gives the lie to the puritanical stringency of the cubes and boxes. Materials are deliberately selected which are not only industrially produced, but, above all, appeal to a rich repertoire of sensual stimuli: colored translucent plexiglass, polished brass, radi-

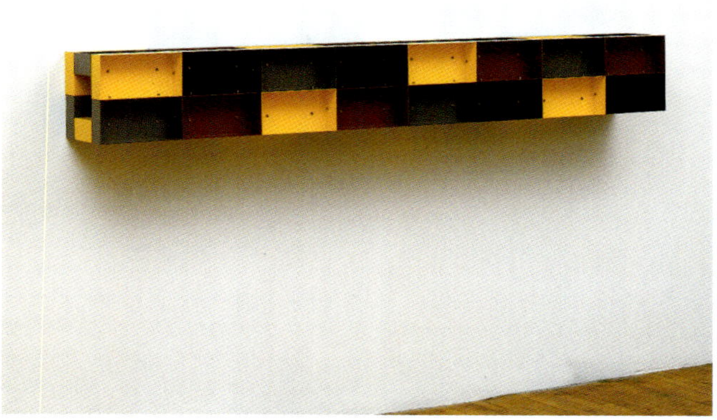

Untitled, 1984, enameled aluminum, 11 7/8" x 141 1/2" x 11 7/8"

ant stainless steel or gleaming mat aluminum are used much more frequently than layered plywood or untreated mat metal. Even without reference to the warm and pleasant sounding "chartreuse anodized aluminum" which Judd used in a wall progression in 1975, it is evident that his use of materials is in the service of a deliberately staged sensual-poetic wealth of associations, which has little in common with the mere sober acknowledgement of them as simply industrial materials with a non-referential objectiveness. Their differentiated colorful transparency and reflectivity are intensified by slight alterations in the strict form, or by surprising inner volumes that have become partially 'charged' in the course of the years with structures; the shadow zones of these volumes – like 'three-dimensional sfumati' – deliberately undermine the clear dimensions of their shell or outer forms. These pictorial means seldom crop up in isolation, but instead determine and intensify one another. Thus the colorfulness of the materials is heightened by reflections, or inner spaces are charged with complex shadow and light structures by the use of simple progressions.

The sensual qualities of Donald Judd's objects as described here are not just restricted to specific work groups or individual phases in his artistic development. They can be made out continually, if with varying intensity, in his whole œuvre since 1964.[2] A quick glance at the catalog of the Judd retrospective exhibition at the New York Whitney Museum of American Art[3] provides an overwhelming impression of the playfully exuberant diversity of his formal and material repertoire, which was carefully extended over the years – a balancing act between continuity and variation, persistence and change, characteristic of Judd's mode of working.

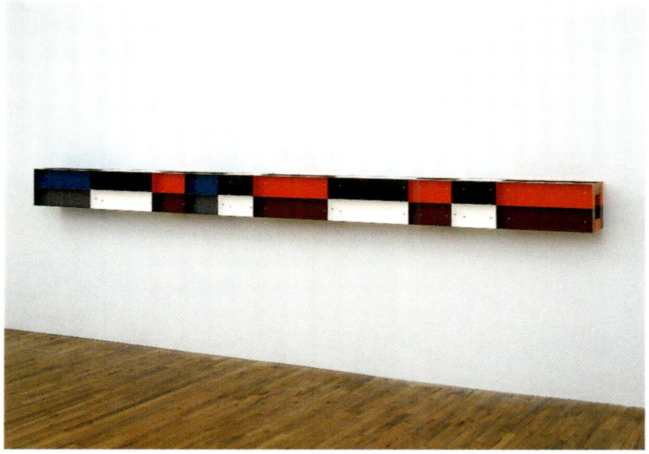

Untitled, 1985, enameled aluminum, 11 7/8" x 177 1/4" x 11 7/8"

Scarcely altered in form or dimension, constantly new formulations of his basic vocabulary emerge, in which neither single-meaninged industrial non-artistic production nor stringent form are manifest. Alongside various individual cube or rectangular works, we encounter, above all, horizontal or vertical progressions: his stacks and his rows of squares or cubes – arranged either at floor level or on the wall, open at the sides or the top, and produced in different materials, colors and measurements – become the basic vocabulary of his works. A diverse artistic vocabulary which by no means retires into sober objectiveness, but instead is aesthetically re-charged in all phases of his work.

This leaning towards sensual, shining surfaces and intriguingly structured internal volumes can be most clearly demonstrated by one outstanding example dated 1991: Judd's contribution to the Klagenfurt exhibition *Shapes and Positions* is an impressive manifestation of the enormous potential which his œuvre draws from the interplay of light and shade, from strongly reflecting surfaces and reduced inner structures: due to their complex filling, the five cubes are no longer immediately comprehensible or clear in structure. Instead, they withdraw from any clear determination (ill. p. 48). Above the row of similar boxes, the inner structures, consisting of three respective supports, allow a second ordering scheme to emerge, which is overlaid on the strict stereometry of the row like a continuous dynamic wave line. The position of the supports, whose volumes are variously formed, is identical in three of the cubes, and reversed as in a mirror image in the two others, namely, the second and fourth.[4] Their 10" diameter provides the basic module for the work, and this recurs in the distance between the cube walls and in the position of the supports. In this way, two in themselves simple and precisely definable ordering systems link to form a complex unity of rhythm and volumes, the elements of which meld with the surrounding inner and outer space into a rich interplay of light and reflection, material and shadows. Instead of clearly defined outlines and structures, what emerge are highly nuanced spaces made up of light and shade, which, given the size and structure of the work, cannot be grasped from a single standpoint: a shimmering interplay between reflecting intermediary and inner spaces, the full extent of which is only perceptible when the observer walks along the rows of cubes.

Is this a totally new Judd then, a Judd of pure sensual exuberance, who has nothing in common with his Minimal Art colleagues? Hardly, especially as this would contribute little towards clarifying what is specifically Minimalist about Donald Judd's art. And not least, because the artist himself can be quoted as a strict opponent of any such 'sensual' reading: in the light of his Philosophy Studies at the New York Columbia University and of his long years of work as an art critic in New York, Judd would seem more than qualified to provide an exact and unassailable location of his œuvre within the history of art.

In an article entitled *Specific Objects*[5] which was published in 1965 and is still read today, if not as a manifesto, then certainly as an essential theoretical text on Minimal Art, Judd, then at the very start of his career, formulated the concept of an art that would develop art objets, "new work", out of modernist painting – works which were neither painting nor sculpture.[6] His claim that "most works finally have one quality" is clearly close to Greenberg's purist thinking in categories of quality and refinement, especially when right before that claim he also remarks that "a work needs only to be interesting."[7] The artists behind these new developments were, alongside Claes Oldenburg and John Chamberlain, above all Barnett Newman and Frank Stella. In addition to its use of industrial materials, the main features of that art, so essentially opposed to the tradition of European art history, are its 'singleness', indivisibility or wholeness, and the resulting objectiveness, as well as the 'real space' of these new works, which consciously integrate three dimensions and thus "get rid of the problem of illusionism."[8] Were one to trust this restrictive – given the above mentioned sensual wealth – definition of what was later known as Minimal Art, then Judd would in fact offer little more than that initially described 'lowest common denominator' of the Minimalists. In this stubborn interpretation, Minimal Art itself degenerated into that late form of modern art which simply translated the stringent pictorial logic of 'formalist' painting into the three-dimensional.

Doubts emerged at an early stage, however, and for a while at least there was great opposition to such a restricted, single-meaninged reading of this new art movement, and in particular of the works of Donald Judd: Richard Wollheim's *Minimal Art* was just one term among many; there was also talk of ABC Art, Pri-

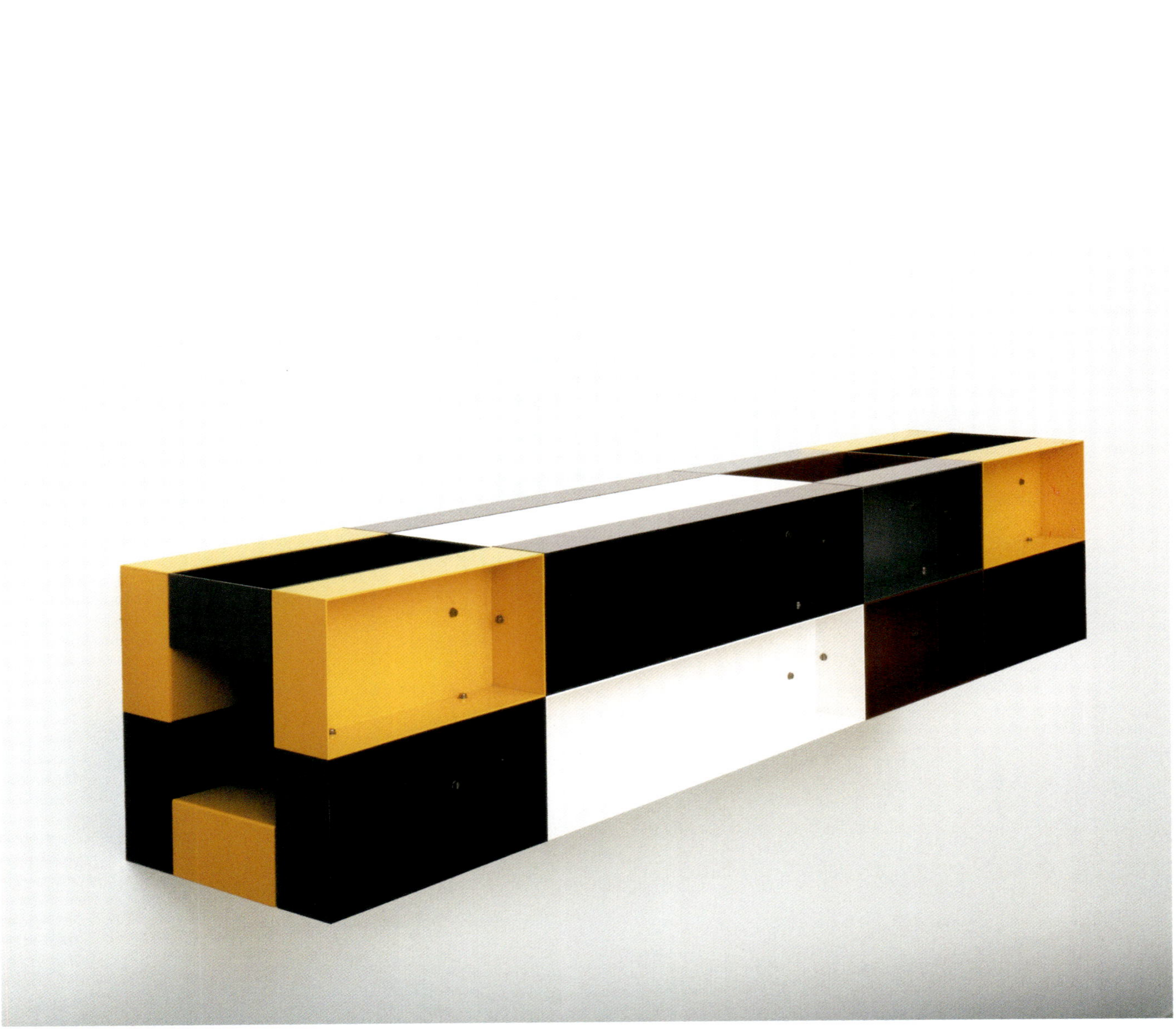

Untitled, 1985, enameled aluminum, 11 7/8" x 59" x 11 7/8" (cat. no. 10)

mary Structures, or Specific Objects, at a time when this apparently fixed canon was being questioned in a more fundamental way than in the decades that followed. Two surprisingly discerning articles published during the formative phase of Minimal Art concentrated on this basic contradiction between stringency and abundance.

In both articles, Judd's œuvre after 1964 was essentially the subject of the authors' deliberations, which are basically opposed to the fundamentals of Minimal Art and which also provide an instructive view of some aspects of his works and their reception during the 60s. Thus as early as 1966, in *Allusion and Illusion in Donald Judd,*[9] Rosalind Krauss emphasized the "unusual beauty" of Judd's recent works and their ability to provoke an experience "that completely transcends the physical object". For her part, Elisabeth Baker, in *Judd the Obscure,*[10] laid particular emphasis on the "sensual qualities" of his works, their "painterly attitude and various pictorial complexities". Both articles have a similar focus, and one which will also be of central importance to our considerations, as it is diametrically opposed to the basic principles of Minimal Art, and in particular to Judd's definition of his 'specific objects'. For both critics, his cubes and boxes, his vertical and horizontal progressions, betray an evident leaning towards 'illusion', which is by no means mere chance or just incidental.

This is a direct and undistorted view of the ambivalent structure of an art which, when thus seen, represents a lot more than just industrial materials, holistic form, and the chauvinistic battle against the history of European art. Unimpeded by the art historical a priori that became established at a later date, the two interpreters had, above all, the possibility of referring explicitly to the cause of this remarkable divergence between their observations and that standardized reception and interpretation which Minimal Art was regularly subjected to at its inception, and even more so in the subsequent years. For Krauss and Baker, the aim was to break the power of a 'theoretical line' which "at least in Judd's case, could (not) measure up to the power of the sculptural position,"[11] and which could basically be traced back to Judd's own writings.[12]

The description given above of a sensual 'Minimalist', therefore, is not just possible in retrospect, meaningful with reference to his late œuvre; it can be presupposed for all his works since the late 1960s. There is an indubitable tension between a deliberately sober and puritanical interpretation of his metals, enamel varnishes or plexiglass surfaces, and the obviously illusionist potential and sensual quality of these materials. And up to this very day, that 'theoretical line', which does not distinguish between polished aluminum and simple steel plates, between colored plexiglass and painted plywood, is still very popular in art history and art criticism. In the reception of his works up until the early 90s, Judd's almost playful handling of light and shade, his highly differentiated surface stimuli, and a deliberate emphasis on the sensual qualities of the selected materials are of almost no significance.

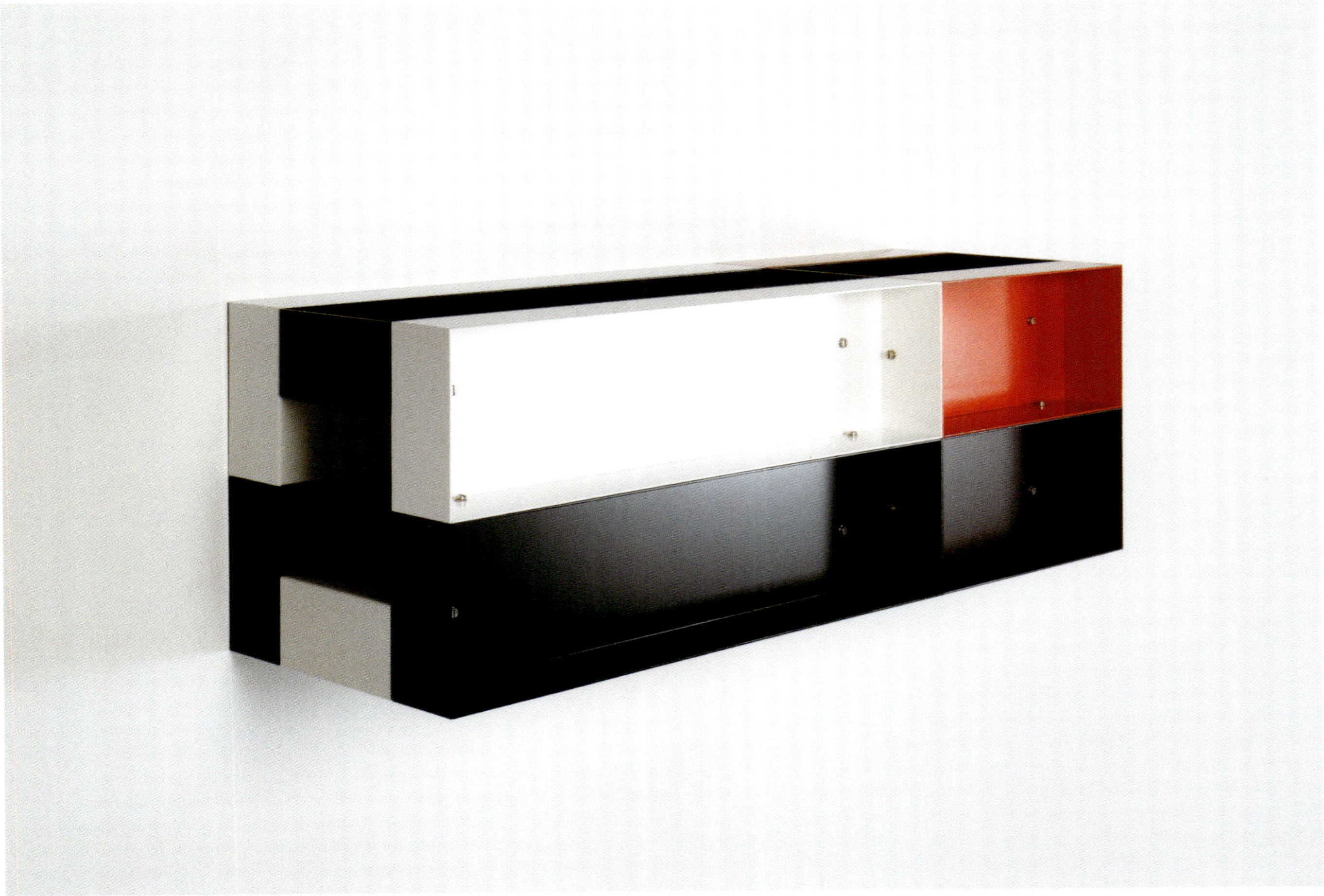

Untitled, 1985, enameled aluminum, 11 7/8" x 35 1/2" x 11 7/8" (cat. no. 8)

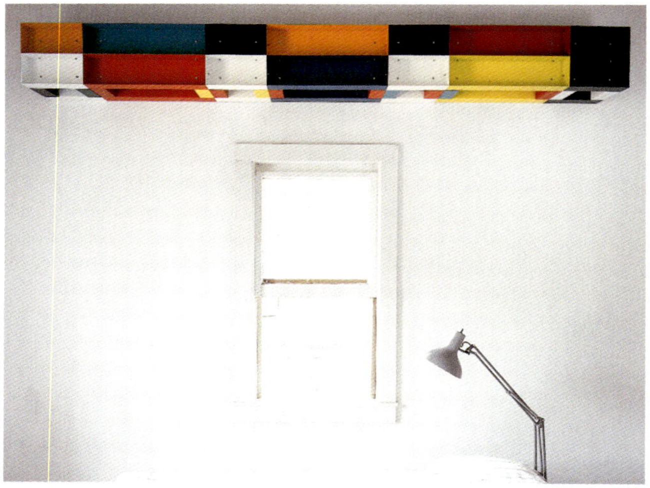

Casa Perez, Ayala de Chinati Ranch, Marfa

Thus in 1988, a good twenty years later, neither the articles, nor the 'illusionist' Judd of these two critics are mentioned, not even in a footnote, in Barbara Haskell's catalog essay[13] for the above mentioned New York Judd retrospective exhibition. Even "illusory (!) surfaces and de-materializing effects" could not question Judd's anti-illusionism and his 'factuality'.[14] Judd remained an unambiguous representative of an art which followed in the footsteps of Greenberg and whose "reduced geometrical forms" illustrated "the modernist demand for a purification of the means."[15] There is an obvious proximity here to Judd's own argumentation in *Specific Objects*, and to a large portion of the existing secondary literature.[16] In 1998, Gregor Stemmrich still sees in Judd's 'specifity' – which for him is the central aspect of his œuvre – merely "a literary version of the modernist concept of the 'essence of medium'."[17] If Judd is read in this way, Stemmrich's "ambiguousness", which turns up in Krauss or Baker as "illusionism" or "pictorial complexities", is avoided by translating painting and its inherent illusionism into 'per se' three-dimensional real objects. Only in the early 90s, with renewed interest in the historical meaning of Minimal Art, were texts published again which acknowledged in more than just a superficial way the illusionism described by Krauss and Baker. This turnabout in the contemporary reception of Judd's works is contained, above all, in *The Inflection* by Yve-Alain Bois,[18] whose excellent interpretation takes the sensual-illusionist aspects of Judd's art seriously.

The tension I referred to above between the strict Minimal rhetoric of art criticism and art history, and the obviously sensual qualities of Judd's works is thus complemented not only by the

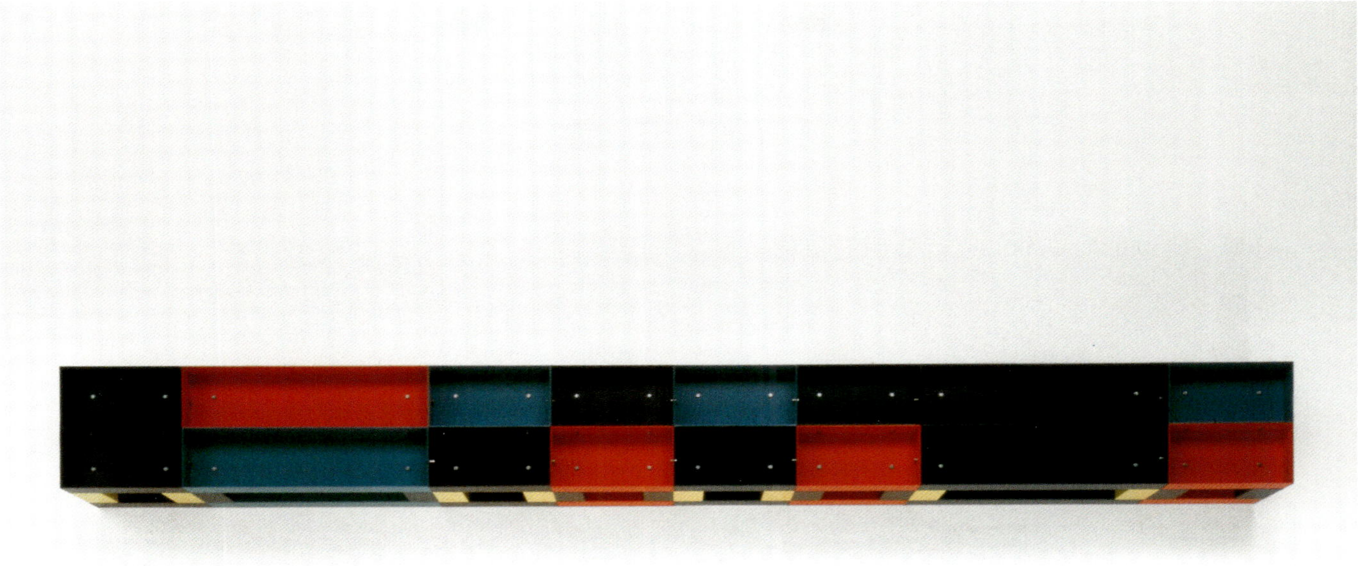

Untitled, 1985, enameled aluminum, 11 7/8" x 118" x 11 7/8" (cat. no. 9)

opposition to these qualities expressed in Judd's early theoretical texts, but also by two resulting and apparently irreconcilable lines of interpretation. I will deal later with the subversive and, as will be shown, ultimately anti-modernist potential of Donald Judd's art, which emerges unavoidably out of an 'illusionist-sensual' reading of his works, and the ambivalent relationship this manifests between Minimal Art and modern art – its tip figure being its completion and overthrow in one.[19] But first it would seem appropriate to turn to Judd's own art theory and its importance for the reception of Minimal Art. In Judd's case, the thesis introduced above of a theory of Minimal art that is only currently in the process of emerging leads, via an examination of the art theory he formulated in his *Specific Objects*, to the unavoidable question of whether and to what extent this early text can be applied to Judd's own art. An important advance towards clarifying and understanding Donald Judd's complex œuvre could be made by a more detailed determination of what is 'specific' about his objects, and by an analysis of his highly consequential text, which perhaps gained access to the reception of Minimal Art too quickly and without adequate consideration.

The complex relationship between the text – which, interestingly enough, is not contained in Gregory Battcock's 1968 anthology of Minimal Art – and Judd's art begins with its dating and continues with an exact determination of its function. On closer observation, there is much to be said against the assumption that *Specific Objects* provides a manifesto-like foundation of Minimal Art, by means of which Judd's art in particular can be grasped in all its complexity. The very range of artists he discusses in this context is much wider than what can be subsumed under the concept of Minimal Art, even in the broadest sense; reference is made to such different artists as Andy Warhol, John Chamberlain and Lee Bontecou; the 'classical' Minimalists like Stella, Flavin and Morris only play a subordinate role. What is more, the latter is mentioned in the same breath as George Brecht, who, according to Judd, is related to the later Minimalists through his use of everyday objects. The author never makes any mention of himself among the approximately fifty names on the list of artists associated in one way or another with his 'specific objects'.[20]

Above all, it is very difficult to establish when exactly the text fits in chronologically. It was first published in autumn 1965 in the New York *Arts Magazine* for which Judd once worked, not very willingly and only until early 1964.[21] At this early point in time, shortly after his first solo exhibition at the New York Green Gallery in 1963, Judd wrote *Specific Objects*, that is to say, more than one year before it was published. This delay in publication is important if one bears in mind that it was then that the decisive change in Judd's range of materials took place: only after writing the text, in the course of 1964, was it possible for him to produce his first metal works and to abandon painted plywood, which he had utilized up till then. What we in retrospect describe as Minimal Art

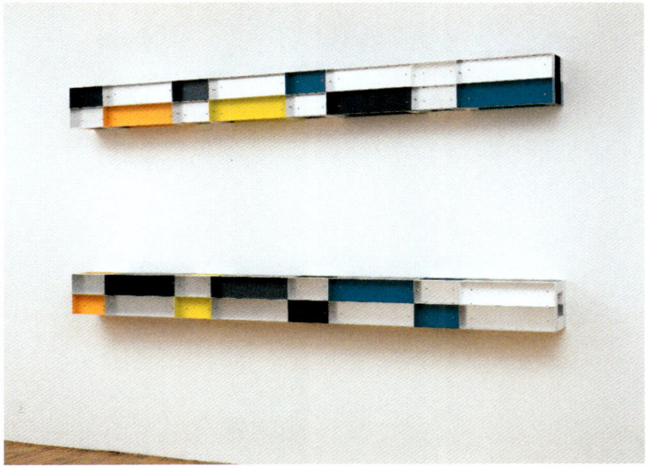

Untitled, 1987, enameled aluminum, 2 units, each 11 7/8" x 141 1/2" x 11 7/8"

was only in its infancy for Judd and the group of Minimal artists in early 1964. Minimal Art exhibitions by the later Minimalists took place only after the text had been written.[22]

The art or artists' group Donald Judd described in the text is not identical with what we today understand under the term Minimal Art, neither from the point of view of time or of personalities. Therefore, *Specific Objects* cannot be read as an inventory, but only as a far-sighted manifesto of that art movement. To put it in another, less prophetically avant-garde way: On closer inspection *Specific Objects* can scarcely be treated as an artist's text that might throw light on the concept and function of Minimal Art, which emerged shortly after it. Judd obviously found it difficult to provide a positive description of the features which distinguished the new 'specific objects' from the art that went before them. The 'singleness' and the belligerent anti-illusionism can easily be deduced from the painting of modernism, but how his 'new work' would extend the concept of formalist painting into a third dimension is not described in detail. Instead there is a list of what the 'new work' cannot or can no longer be. But how the new 'real space' that emerges from painterly anti-illusionism differs from traditional or contemporary sculptural space is no more clear than the question as to how the objectiveness put forward in this text is derived from the 'singleness' of the painting of Newman or Pollock.

Judd bridged a gap in his theoretical argumentation by listing a hoard of examples, which for the most part originated in the New York art scene and had one thing in common: they were all a long way from the 'new work' and its vaguely described 'specificity'.

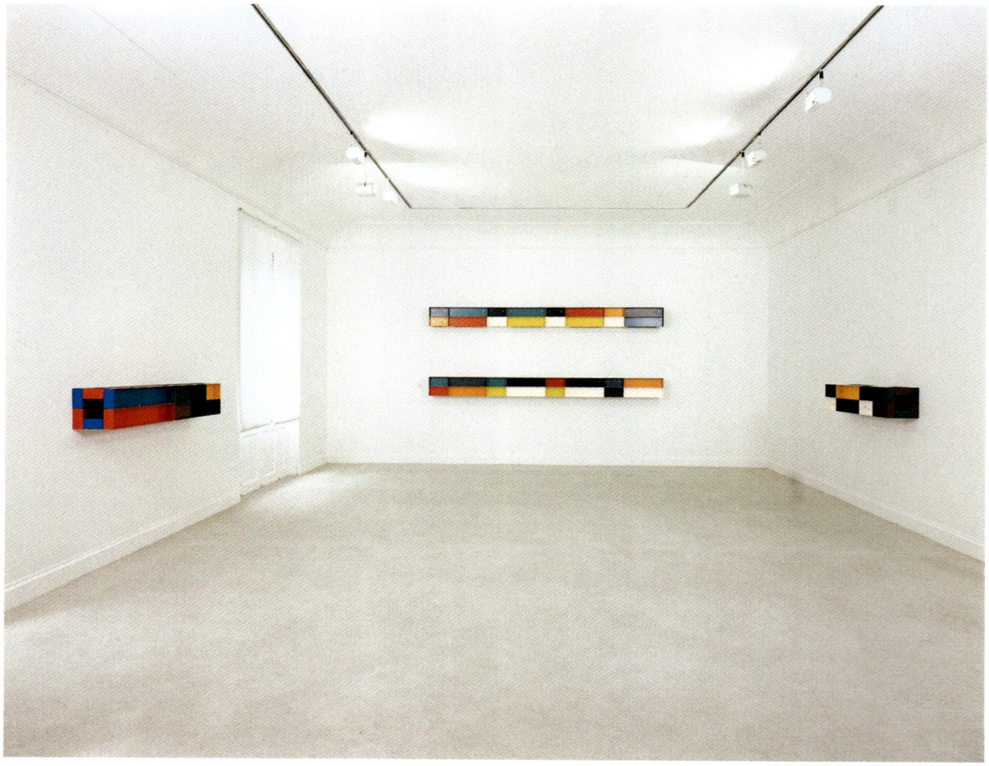

Installation, Galerie Lelong, Paris 1987

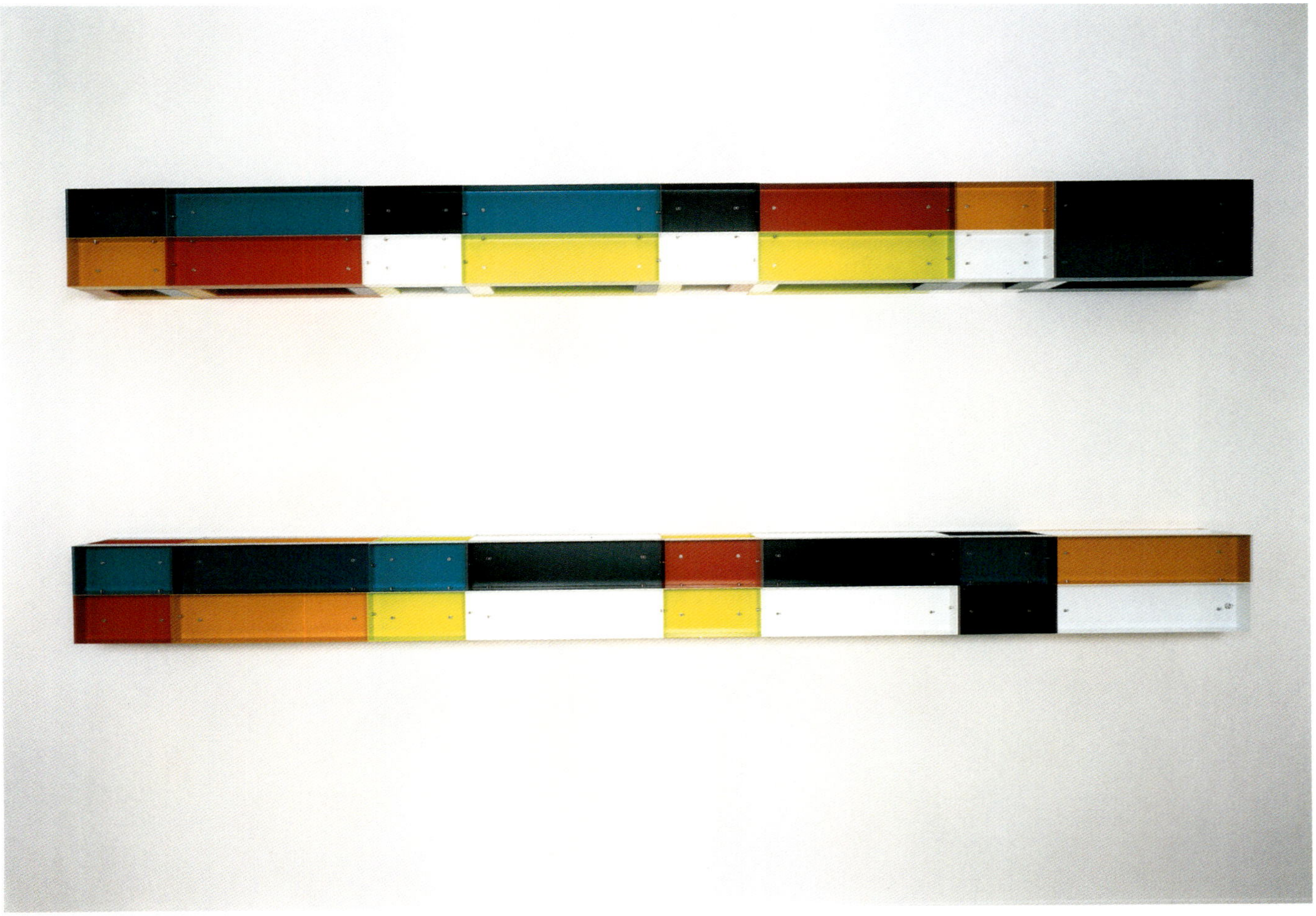

Untitled, 1987, enameled aluminum, 2 units, each 11 7/8" x 141 1/2" x 11 7/8" (cat. no. 11)

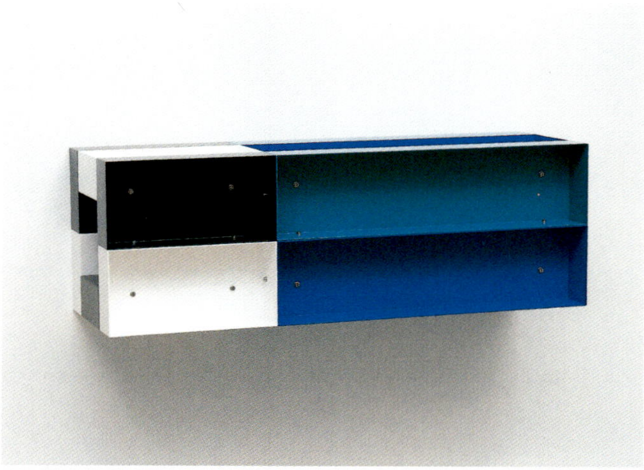

Untitled, 1989, enameled aluminum, 11 7/8" x 35 1/2" x 11 7/8"

Only Claes Oldenburg and his vinyl objects were considered adequate for describing the concept behind the 'specific objects' and all their features. Judd devoted particular attention to Oldenburg on account of his 'specific' and 'direct' use of industrial materials. In his case alone do the – also only vaguely defined – 'new' spatiality of his objects, the use of industrial materials, and a new 'singleness' combine to produce Judd's 'specific objects'. This trend towards the 'holistic' object, however, can hardly be derived from the formalism of the 1950s. This 'real space' and its new objectiveness cannot be grasped through a new definition of the spatial context, but rather through its proximity to the objects of everyday life. Industrial materials are not simply utilized, with these new materials anti-illusionist everyday objects are produced which reject the representative aspects of traditional art in a very different way to that demonstrated by the painting of Newman or Stella. The apparently so central concept of 'real space', which accounted for the later fame of *Specific Objects*, is defined neither in a new way, nor in its difference to traditional sculptural space. Instead, recourse is had to a new way of anchoring the art object in everyday life. Judd's 'real space', as defined in *Specific Objects*, has nothing in common with the experience of space described earlier in the context of Judd's objects, and which, since Krauss' article, has been closely associated with the phenomenology of Maurice Merleau-Ponty. In general, no attention is paid to the observer and his new active part within the framework of a concept of the art work based on openness and incompletion. What is more, this new perception, which critically reflects the work's autonomy, is due essentially to identical objects being arranged in rows, a central aspect of Minimal Art to which Judd attributes no importance whatsoever in his theoretical foundation of Minimal Art.

Judd only hints at his own use of new industrial materials – which comes close to that of Minimal Art – and at their still endless possibilities, when he mentions Flavin's fluorescent tubing, or lists, as examples among other things, aluminum, brass or plexiglass, all of which play an essential role in his own later work. Otherwise there is little in *Specific Objects* that might be of anything more than superficial relevance for Judd's Minimal Art. The derivation of his 'specific objectiveness' from the formalist painting of the 1950s may, under certain circumstances, be of enormous importance for his art, but it is confusing in the context of this text. The art he lists as exemplary, from Oldenburg to Lee Bontecou and Andy Warhol to John Chamberlain, has only little in common with the 'lowest common denominator' of Minimal Art mentioned earlier, to say nothing of the reading of Judd as sensual-illusionist, for which I have a preference.

The cadmium red plywood works which Judd exhibited at the New York Green Gallery before writing the article are the only ones to betray a similar proximity to the object and the banal reality of the everyday described in *Specific Objects*. Judd's subsequent success, which then allowed him to use new materials, lies exactly between the writing and the publication of the article, and thus not only expresses his breakthrough as an artist, but above all a radical break in his œuvre. It speaks for itself, therefore, that the term 'specific object', which along with many others still survives today in the context of Minimal Art, is not used by Judd himself anymore after 1964, at least not in his writings. If one wants to ascribe a significance to *Specific Objects* within Judd's œuvre, then one must acknowledge that the text is certainly not oriented towards the stereometric works in plexiglass and aluminum that he produced after writing it, but refers back to his early plywood works and their respective mixed New York ambience – between Newman and Neo-Dada.[23]

The driving force of his art after 1964 can be located in the very ambivalence that exists between formalism and reality, and that is such an essential feature of the early text. In view especially of its manner of arguing 'ex negativo' over large stretches, *Specific Objects* is to be read not so much as a text on Minimal Art, as has been assumed to date, but more profitably as a description of an obvious deficit, a lack of perspective in the art of the late 1950s. With its sensually broken objectiveness, Donald Judd's art goes far beyond the 'late modern' object character of *Specific Objects* and formulates a totally new aspiration to reality, though without taking the diversion via the aesthetic of everyday objects which the text makes reference to. The artistic translation, however, differs greatly from the theoretical one: the none too helpful opposition hinted at in the text between formalism and the Duchamp readymade arrives at a surprising synthesis in his works after 1964.

The key to understanding the contradictions and ambiguities in Judd's œuvre and 'fortuna critica' lies ultimately in an exact determination of his artistic position at the end of modernism. Doubtless, Judd developed essential aspects of the objectiveness of his Minimal Art from the rhetoric of formalism, and thus took an art theory developed for and through examples of American painting in the 1950s into the third dimension – although, or rather because he regarded painting 'per se' as outmoded and no longer appropriate. The result of this creative transformation process, however, has as little in common with the 'new work' in *Specific Objects* as with the formalism of the 1950s, which can be easily demonstrated by his blurring of the apparently established concepts, his anti-illusionism, or his demand for 'real space'.

If the aim of the painting Judd envisaged to was to achieve clarity and stringency by avoiding a traditional painterly spatiality, he himself proceeded to turn this painterly anti-illusionism into its sculptural opposite, a turnabout which was, of course, already anticipated in the striving towards planarity evident in the painting of 1950s: if space disappears from the picture, the picture becomes an object in space. And the supposed end point of painting, formulated by Stella in his "what you see is what you see", is exposed as outmoded by the step into the third dimension. Judd's art insists on the importance of such a re-defined third dimension and the associated dependence on the surrounding space. Like painting's rigid formal recourse to the square canvas, which both constitutes and restricts it, space in Judd's Minimal Art is both the condition and the extension of his work. Without the legacy of formalism, its formal stringency, its wholeness, and its rejection of any hierarchical order, Judd can thus emphasize the central quality of his three-dimensional works: their aspiration to non-mediated, directly 'tangible' reality.

In both cases, the austere exterior form, the element of reduction, is the precondition for the genesis of new relationships that point to a reality beyond the picture: a moment of extreme reduction, which here leads to a new abundance. When all innerpictorial relations are exhausted, art turns outwards, to new external references, its dependence on reality. This is a tendency that Judd deliberately intensifies and veritably stages, when he deliberately undermines the stereometric forms by more or less complex internal structures and strongly reflecting surfaces, or when the 'minimalist' progressions in no way serve to acknowledge identical stereometric givens, but the exact opposite: both strategies direct the observer's attention to the inconsistency in his perception of formally identical parts. These severe sober shell forms allow Judd to treat light and color, surfaces and reflections with playful freedom, a treatment which develops its fundamental quality in the tense opposition between material and form, identity and difference.

Two perceptions, true in themselves but irreconcilably contradictory, become superimposed without fully agreeing. The process of

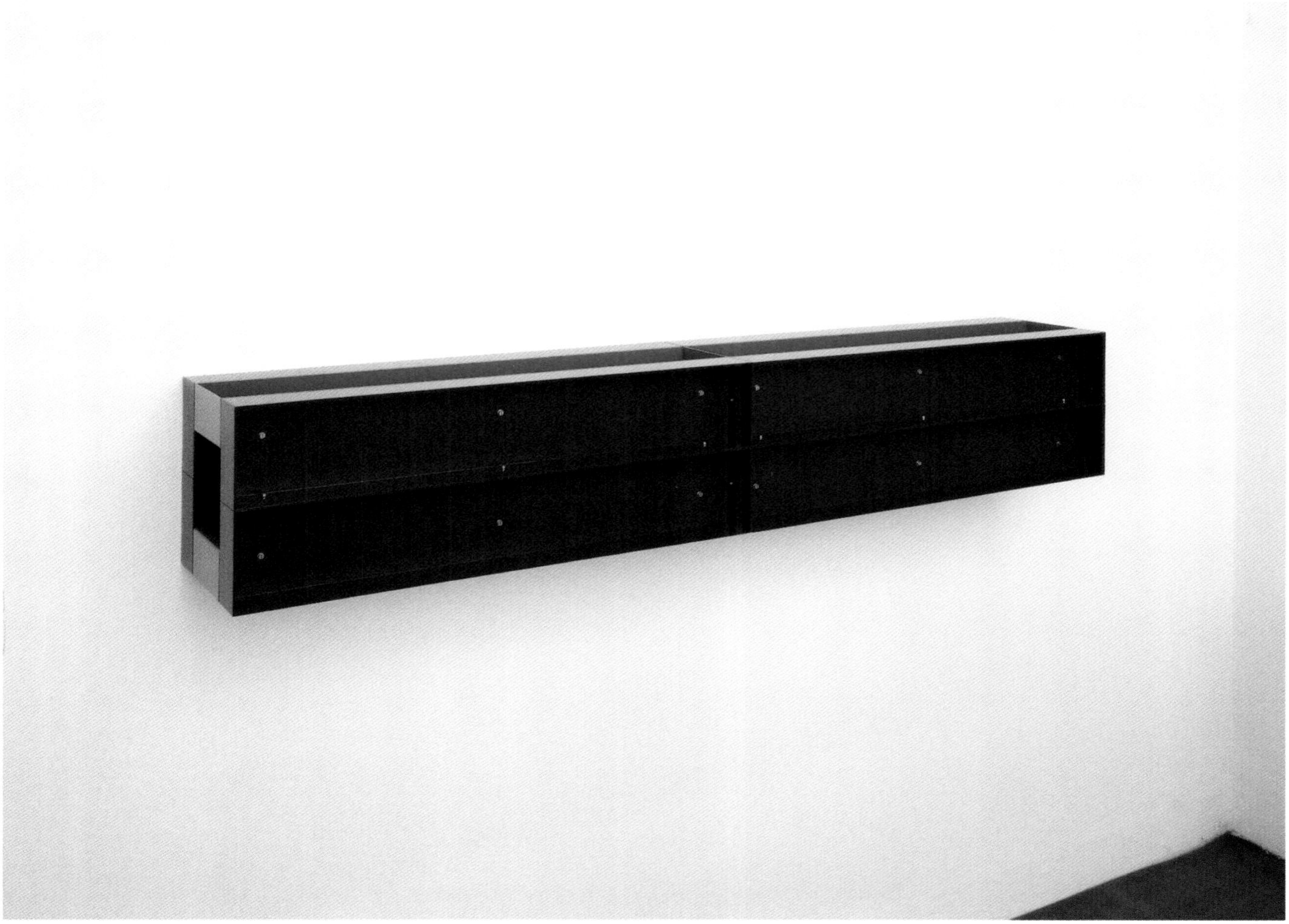

Untitled, 1989, enameled aluminum, 11 7/8" x 70 7/8" x 11 7/8" (cat. no. 14)

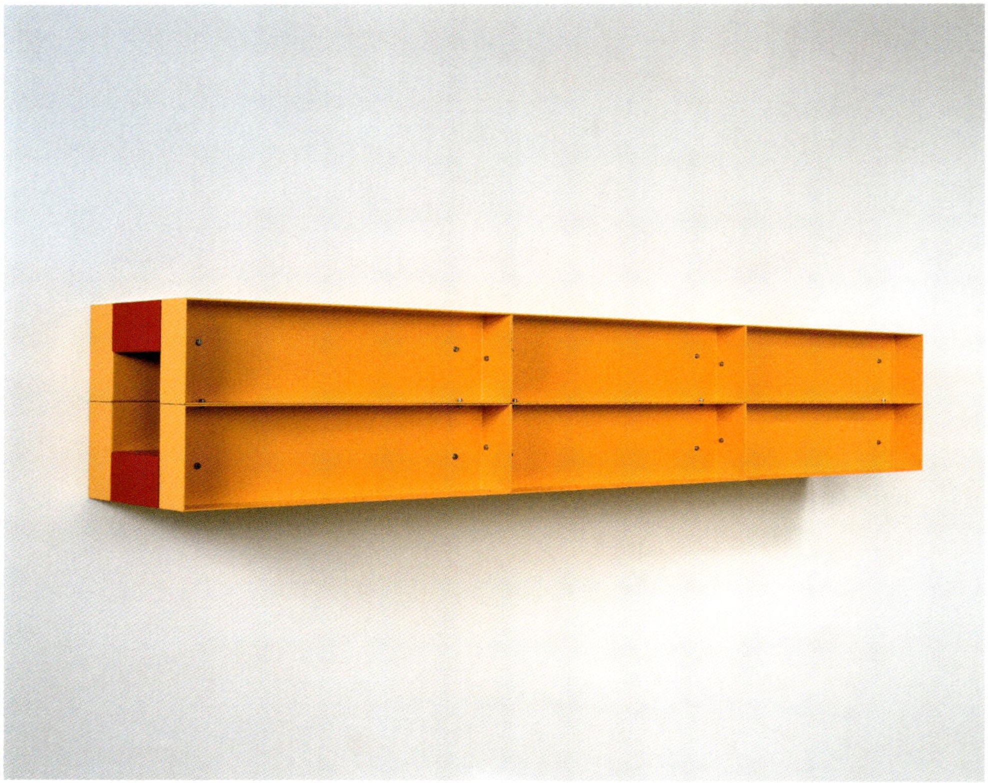

Untitled, 1989, enameled aluminum, 11 7/8“ x 70 7/8“ x 11 7/8“ (cat. no. 13)

Ill. p. 71: **Untitled, 1989, enameled aluminum, 11 7/8“ x 70 7/8“ x 11 7/8“ (cat. no. 15)**

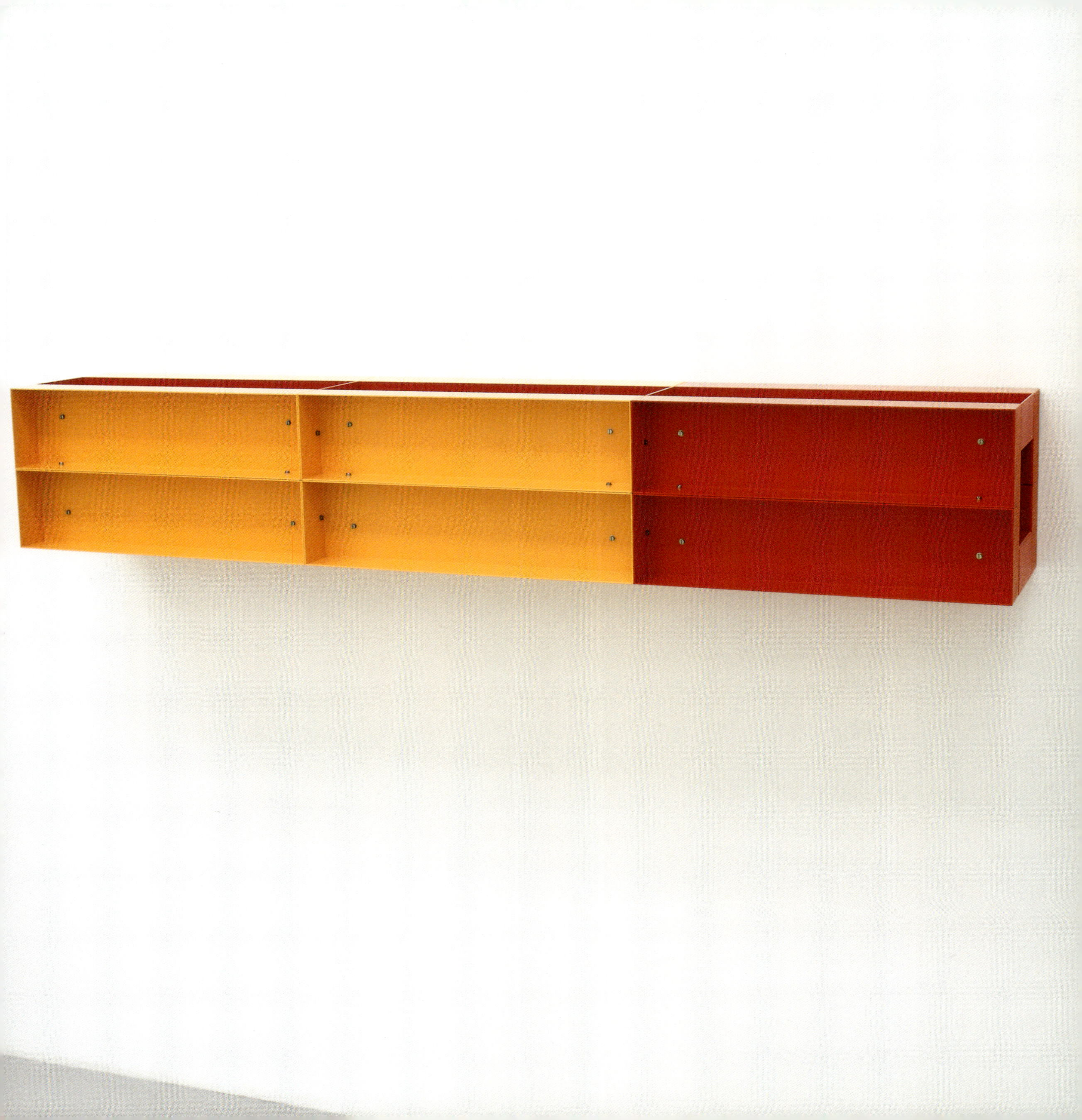

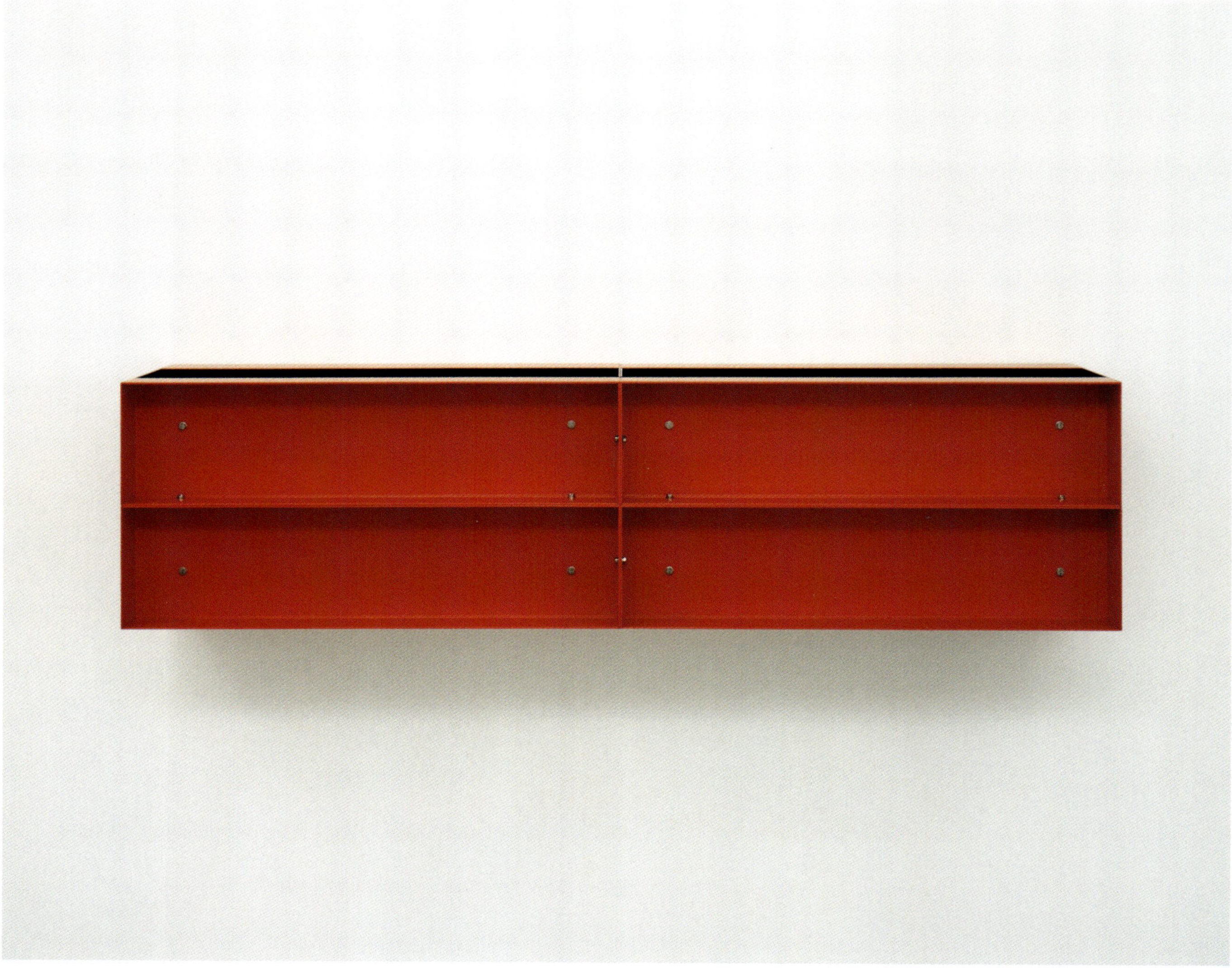

Untitled, 1989, enameled aluminum, 11 7/8" x 47 1/2" x 11 7/8"

reception has a dual dynamism, a parallel movement: along with the observer, who has to walk along the work and enter in various ways, even physically, into a relationship with it, there is also the approach to the content, the meaningful linking of various levels ranging from extreme rationality to exuberant emotion. Two contrasting and complementary movements, which determine and intensify one another, integrating the observer into a choreographic context that effects both body and soul – the goal being not so much the objectifiable completeness as the dynamic openness of the work.

Yet Judd's art loses what Greenberg and his school held most dearly: its autonomy. Although his art conjures up an aura of precious inviolability around its shining and colorfully shimmering materials, the gesture of auratic untouchableness[24] becomes transformed into its opposite: While Judd's objects would seem to reject any haptic appropriation on the part of the observer, they transform him and his real surroundings into an integral part of the work through the extrovert sensuality of the surfaces and the ambiguity of their inner spaces. That his vehement anti-illusionism, which takes the logic of formalism to its extreme, turns into a sensual illusionism is one of the surprising imponderables of art history, above and beyond artists' manifestos, theories, and statements. It is then not far of course to Merleau-Ponty, his "lived perspective" and the physical perception of art. In such a phenomenological interpretation, perception becomes the sum of an endless number of different perspectives, and seeing an object becomes an endless process that will never give rise to a last, or generally valid perception. This is a line of interpretation that Krauss was the first to put forward in her text on Judd cited above, though only to illustrate it with reference to Robert Morris' *L-Beams*.[25] With their stringently sober exterior surface, Morris' equal sided right angles made of painted plywood are obviously better suited to translating Merleau-Ponty's phenomenology into art than Judd's complex sensual objects. But sensuality, the non-rational, physical perception, are neglected in Morris' theoretically exemplary translation. (To say nothing of the complexity and contradictoriness of Merleau-Ponty's philosophy, which is scarcely to be found in the simplified artistic adaptation.) Judd's sensual abundance has little in common with Morris' didactic approach. Even if both consciously question the identity of their objects in the permanence of the process of sensual perception, Judd deliberately emancipates himself from the mere acknowledgement of a philosophical fact. The specific relevance of recourse to philosophy is considerably diminished, for example, when with reference to Krauss and Benjamin H. D. Buchloh, Briony Fer describes Judd as "exemplary for the phenomenological concern of Minimalism", while at the same time admitting that Michael Fried, an ardent opponent of Minimal Art and its – in the final analysis phenomenological – 'theatricality' is entitled to quote the same philosopher, this time positively, for the work of Anthony Caro.[26]

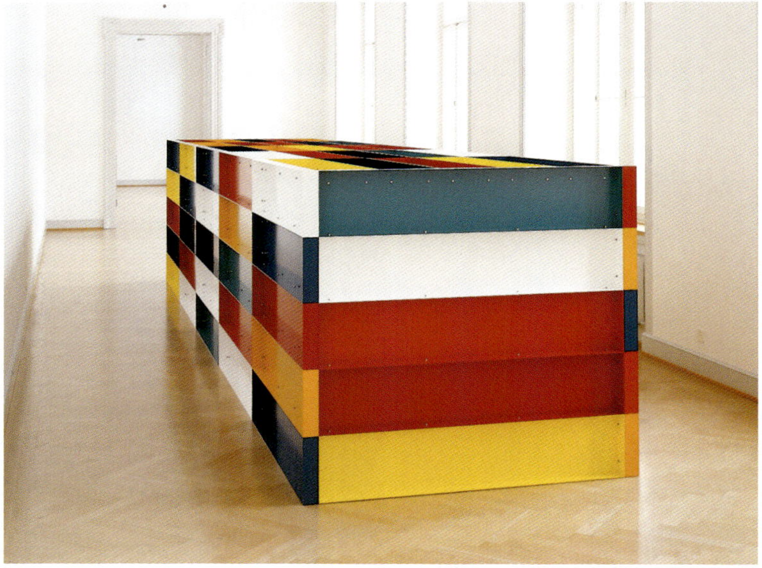

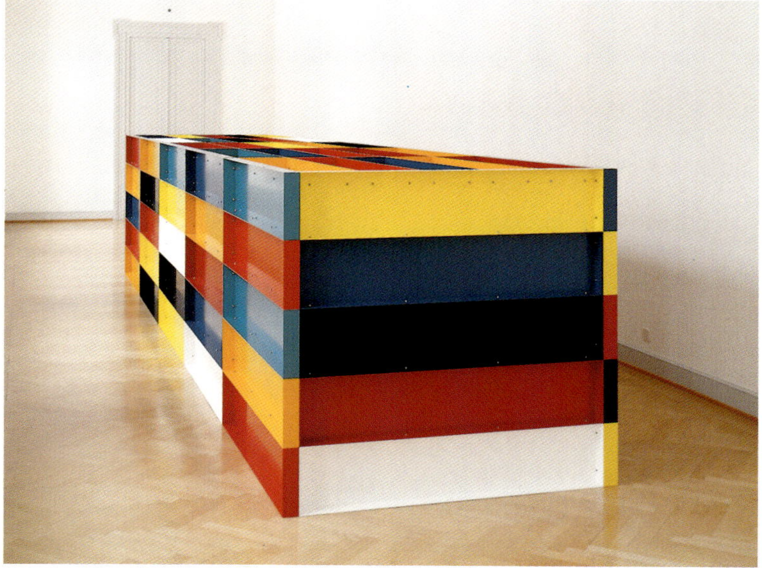

Untitled, 1991, enameled aluminum, 59" x 64" x 295"

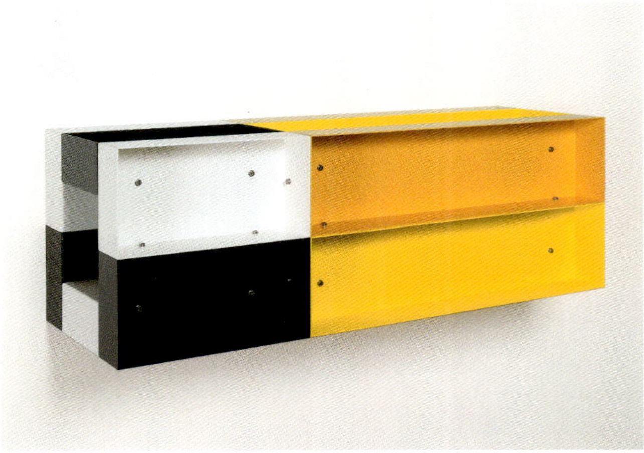

Untitled, 1989, enameled aluminum, 11 7/8" x 35 1/2" x 11 7/8"

The importance of Donald Judd's Minimal Art, therefore, can be only partially explained by its proximity to the phenomenology of Merleau-Ponty,[27] or by its broad-scale new definition of central art terms, such as space, movement or illusion, and more adequately by its capacity to give a credible artistic form to the interface between the modern and the post-modern, the emergence of the neo-avantgardes.[28] When, for example, Stephan Schmidt-Wulffen locates the crack in the core of minimalist self-understanding (which for him is identical with the cited 'lowest common denominator' of Minimal Art) in the impossibility of bringing about an identity between idea and object, and when for him formalist-minimalist 'literalness' turns out to be impossible,[29] then Judd replies not as a theoretician, but by celebrating that crack in each of his works and allowing it to be the creative potential of his art. One cannot really speak of the failure of Minimalism, as diagnosed by Schmidt-Wulffen. On the contrary, in Judd's gleaming and reflecting metal squares and colorful translucent plexiglass surfaces the consequences of the breach between the neo-avantgarde and modernism become physically and sensually tangible as a breach which leads directly to the overwhelming abundance of an extended concept of art. Thus in the process of their perception, in the slow unfolding of their aesthetic complexity, each of Donald Judd's works can be read as a paradigm of that fundamental and still extremely forceful reorientation of art in the post-war era.

From the German by Pauline Cumbers

Notes

1 The ideas put forward here were first formulated for my Master's thesis of 1995 on Donald Judd's art and art theory. They were recently expanded on for a lecture at the Hallen für Neue Kunst in Schaffhausen, and reworked yet again for this article. I would like to take this opportunity of thanking Kira van Lil, Schaffhausen, Annina Zimmermann, Basel, and Volker Bauermeister, Freiburg, for important suggestions, stimulating discussions, and a critical perusal of this manuscript.

2 The previous paintings and the three-dimensional works made of painted cadmium red plywood, which Judd showed in 1963 at the Green Gallery, are being excluded here for the moment. It is out of this tension between his early works before 1964 and his Minimalist major works after that date that I will be deducing essential aspects of his œuvre.

3 Barbara Haskell, *Donald Judd: Beyond Formalism*, in *Donald Judd* (cat.), Whitney Museum of American Art, New York 1988, pp. 17–114.

4 This is the only real change in Judd's formal vocabulary after 1964. In the early 80s, he produced the first works which, unlike the wall and floor progressions of the 60s and 70s, no longer repeat identical forms, but instead fill the otherwise empty inner spaces with, as a rule, non-identical inner volumes. The one hundred aluminum works in Marfa (1980–84; ill. p. 45) and the exhibits at the Baden-Baden exhibition (1989; ill. pp. 94–97) are referred to here as outstanding examples. Interestingly enough, it is this, to my mind, only progression of identical inner volumes – Untitled, 1977, six plywood cubes open at the front and back, with horizontal walls running diagonally from right to left and dividing up the inner space – exhibited in Otterlo in 1980 on which Yve-Alain Bois bases his new view of Judd's œuvre and at the same time ascertains a fundamental change in that œuvre. Bois' Text (*Die Wandlung*, in *Shapes and Positions* (cat.), Ritter Kunsthalle, Klagenfurt 1992, pp. 33–51), which is central to the reception of Judd's work, has also been a source of essential insight for this examination of Judd, although I disagree with it as regards the assumed "inflection", i.e., a break in his formal repertoire. For example, the "artist's change of course in terms of the factor of light", which Bois sees in the early 70s (p. 38), is untenable; light and shadow played an essential role in Judd's œuvre since the mid-60s.

5 Donald Judd, *Specific Objects*, in *Arts Yearbook*, No. 8, 1965, pp. 74–82. Reprint in *Complete Writings 1959–1975*, Halifax/New York 1975, pp. 181–189.

6 Judd began as a painter, and his early works are clearly in the context of American painting of the 50s. The use of color and form always bears witness to this legacy of his early painting, if often to varying degrees.

7 Donald Judd, *Specific Objects*, in *Complete Writings 1959–1975*, Halifax/ New York 1975, p. 184. Here he places his art in a new critical and self-reflective context, and takes leave of modernism's thinking in terms of progress. At the same time, we already see here a certain blurring of the terms used by Judd, to which I will devote more attention later.

8 Donald Judd, *Specific Objects*, in *Complete Writings 1959–1975*, Halifax/New York 1975, p. 184.

9 Rosalind Krauss, *Allusion and Illusion in Donald Judd*, in *Artforum*, May 1966, pp. 24–26.

10 Elisabeth Baker, *Judd the Obscure*, in *Art News*, April 1968, pp. 44/45, 60–62.

11 Rosalind Krauss, *Allusion and Illusion in Donald Judd*, in *Artforum*, May 1966, p. 24.

12 Cf. Elisabeth Baker, *Judd the Obscure*, in *Art News*, April 1968, p. 44.

13 Barbara Haskell, *Donald Judd: Beyond Formalism*, in *Donald Judd* (cat.), Whitney Museum of American Art, New York 1988, pp. 17–114. Haskell neglects, however, to show to what extent Judd's œuvre might be interpreted through her reading as an overcoming of formalism, which the title implies. However, her statements in *The Vision Extended: Marfa, Texas* (pp.117–124), which interestingly enough are placed after her catalog text as a separate article, extend the horizon beyond the established narrow formalist framework, when she claims: "Yet he has also moved beyond (!) the narrowly perceived confines of the Minimalist style with which he was initially (!) identified to create a richly varied and lyric vocabulary." Yet two resulting essential questions remain unanswered: In which direction and to what extent does Judd's Minimalist style change, and are her observations, evidently so closely linked with Marfa, usefully applicable to Judd's complete œuvre and his wide range of materials?

14 Barbara Haskell, *Donald Judd: Beyond Formalism*, in *Donald Judd* (cat.), Whitney Museum of American Art, New York 1988, p. 73. She deliberately does not use illusionistic, but instead illusory, which is less problematic in the context of Judd's art theory.

15 Barbara Haskell, *Donald Judd: Beyond Formalism*, in *Donald Judd* (cat.), Whitney Museum of American Art, New York 1988, p. 17. And even more clearly: "... makes his (Judd's) criticism now appear an extension rather than a break with modernism" (p. 81).

16 Both Roberta Smith's essay in the complete catalog of the works until 1974 (*Donald Judd*, in *Donald Judd* (Catalogue Raisonné), National Gallery of Canada, Ottawa 1975, pp. 3–31), and Frances Colpitt's survey of Minimal Art (*Minimal Art. The Critical Perspective*, Seattle 1992), plus Edward Strickland's investigations into the roots of Minimalism in art and music (*Minimalism: origins*, Bloomington 1993) discuss Judd mainly in the context of Greenberg's presence, its aesthetic autonomy and inaccessibility to the observer.

17 Gregor Stemmrich, *Grundkonzepte der Minimal Art*, in *Minimal Maximal. Die Minimal Art und ihr Einfluß auf die internationale Kunst der 90er Jahre*, Museum Weserburg, Bremen 1998, p. 14. Stemmrich's "literalist space" implies a reflection on the relationship between real space and illusory space, which defines illusionism as a necessary aspect of reality. Thus illusion would be a kind of by-product of every act of perception. Such an incidentalness in the context of perception, which we can discern in Robert Morris, fails to fully describe Judd's empathic illusionism. Whether this reversal can be helpful in accessing Judd's specific illusionism will be dealt with in more detail in the following.

18 Yve-Alain Bois, *Die Wandlung*, in *Shapes and Positions* (cat.), Ritter Kunsthalle, Klagenfurt 1992, pp. 33–51. First published as *The Inflection*, in *Donald Judd. New Sculpture* (cat.), The Pace Gallery, New York 1991, unpag.

19 Cf. Hal Foster, *Die Crux des Minimalismus*, in *Shapes and Positions* (cat.), Ritter Kunsthalle, Klagenfurt 1992, p. 149.

20 On the contrary, on the occasion of the first print of his writings (*Complete Writings 1959–1975*, Halifax/New York 1975) Judd laid great store by the editorial remark that the editor, and not he himself, had added a photograph of one of his works. Nevertheless, he valued the text highly and had it included again in the second volume of his writing, from 1975–1986 (*Complete writings 1975–1986*, Stedelijk van Abbemuseum, Eindhoven 1987).

21 "I wrote criticism as a mercenary and would never have written it otherwise", wrote Judd in the foreword to Complete Writings 1959–1975 (Halifax/New York 1975, p. VII). As soon as he could, he discontinued his activities as an art critic. *Specific Objects* is one of the very few longer articles which Judd was able to publish. In this context, he himself speaks of concessions made to the editor. Judd's style has been justifiably described as ponderous and formally descriptive by Colpitt (*Minimal Art. The Critical Perspective*, Seattle 1992, p. 4), and by Haskell (*Donald Judd: Beyond Formalism*, in *Donald Judd* (cat.), Whitney Museum of American Art, New York 1988, p. 81). Scarcely any philosophical conceptual remarks, which one might expect given the reputation of the artist-critic, are to be found in his text.

22 If one accepts Colpitt's list of exhibitions in the context of Minimal Art, then before 1964 the only relevant entries are for Judd and Morris (*Minimal Art. The Critical Perspective*, Seattle 1992, p. 2, 197–199). Whereas Morris' group exhibition at the Green Gallery mainly showed "Neo-Dada-works" (Colpitt), the few stereometric objects also included in the exhibition are obviously connected with his early performances. In any case, Judd also discusses – though without enthusiasm – these proto-minimal works (*Complete Writings 1959–1975*, Halifax/New York 1975, p. 90), yet does not refer to those painted plywood works in *Specific Objects*. He does however mention Morris in the same breath as George Brecht (!). Whether Judd's own exhibition at the same gallery belongs in the context of Minimal Art is an open question.

23 Significantly, in Gregor Stemmrich's anthology the text is preceded by an installation photograph of the Green Gallery exhibition (*Minimal Art. Eine kritische Retrospektive*, Dresden/Basel 1995, p. 58). Also of great interest is the list of artists, who are scarcely know anymore today, yet who are mentioned with illustrations in the first collection of Judd's writings: the objects by H. C. Westermann, Robert Watts, John Anderson or Yayoi Kusama are in fact "objects without a function ... with a Dadaist-Surrealist side to them", as Bois describes (*Die Wandlung*, in *Shapes and Positions* (cat.), Ritter Kunsthalle, Klagenfurt 1992, p. 35), though actually with reference to Judd's cadmium red works.

24 Along with Bois, Briony Fer (*Judd's Specific Objects*, in Briony Fer, *On Abstract Art*, New Haven/London 1997, pp. 131–151) is one of the few critics who in his attempt to re-evaluate his œuvre refers to Judd's sensual qualities. On the basis of observations which come close to those made here, he, however, develops a psychoanalytical reading, which makes out a phantasmatic dimension between pleasure and anxiety, sensual attraction and untouchability. Fer only makes passing reference to the fact that the haptic refusal he describes is compensated by other strategies.

25 Cf. Rosalind Krauss, *Passages in Modern Sculpture*, London 1977, pp. 266/267. Generally speaking, she now claims that illusionism has no significance in the context of Minimal Art. The powerful critical potential concealed within this term, especially as regards Judd's œuvre, is not important anymore in her interpretation.

26 Cf. Briony Fer, *Judd's Specific Objects*, in Briony Fer, *On Abstract Art*, New Haven/London 1997, p. 136, note 18.

27 It remains to be seen whether the *Phenomenology of Perception*, which first appeared in an English translation in the early 60s, must be regarded as being of such great relevance for the genesis of Minimal Art, as is often claimed. For Judd in particular it must be acknowledged, that the œuvre of the supposed artist-philosopher would be only inadequately described with reference to the French phenomenologist.

28 Cf. Hal Foster, *Die Crux des Minimalismus*, in *Shapes and Positions* (cat.), Ritter Kunsthalle, Klagenfurt 1992, p. 160.

29 Cf. Stephan Schmidt-Wulffen, *Den Minimalismus vergessen...!*, in *Minimal Maximal* (cat.), Museum Weserburg, Bremen 1998, pp. 59–62. His negative, as only formalist, view of Minimal Art, which in essential features is surprisingly reminiscent of Haskell's Judd interpretation, is only weakened in a subordinate clause, in which he too sees the progressiveness of Minimal Art in the fact that it "reads Merleau-Ponty".

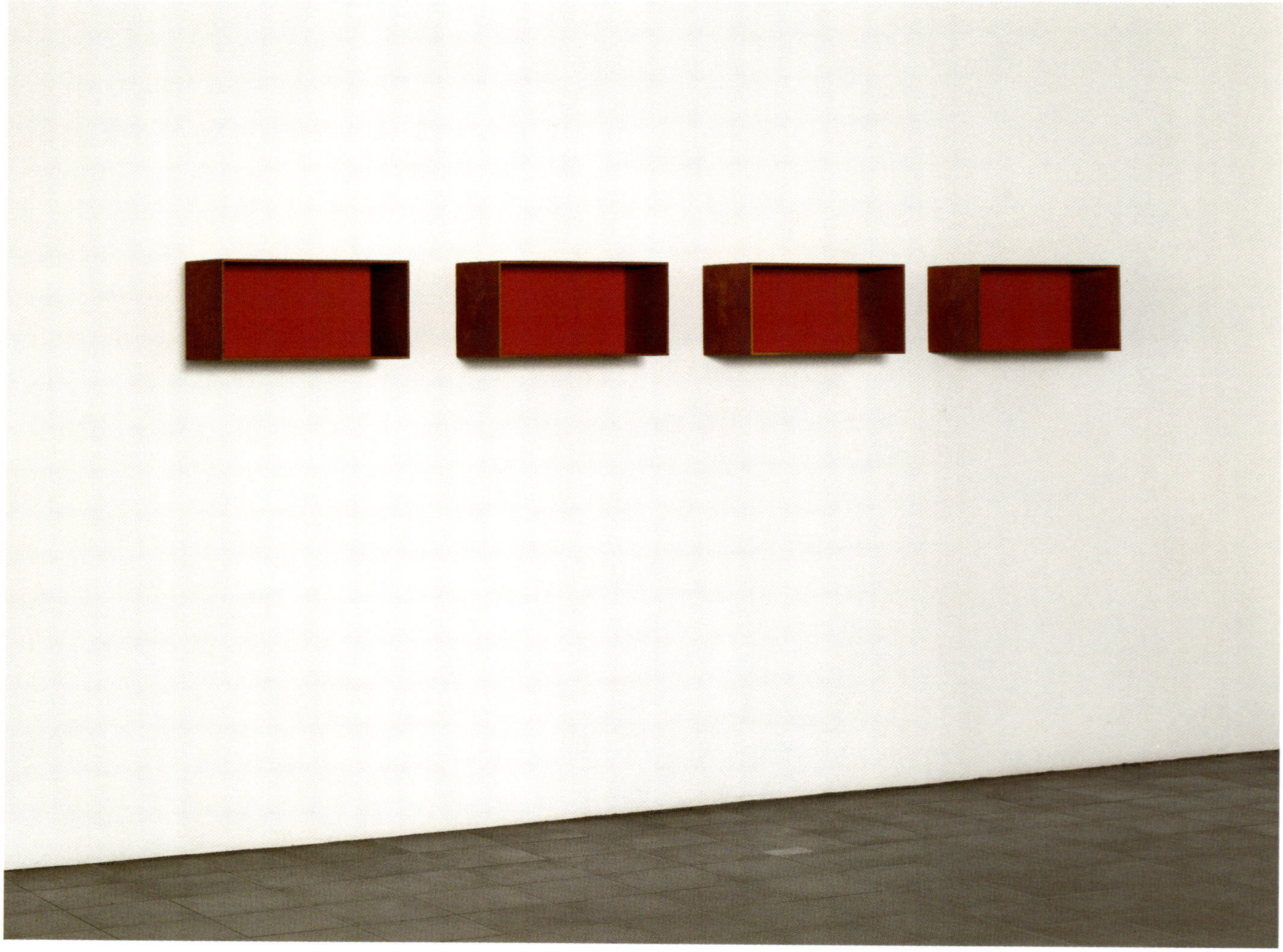

Untitled, 1989, Cor-ten steel, plexiglass, 4 units, each 9 7/8" x 19 5/8" x 9 7/8" (cat. no. 17)

Some aspects of color in general and red and black in particular (1993)

Donald Judd

Material, space, and color are the main aspects of visual art. Everyone knows that there is material that can be picked up and sold, but no one sees space and color. Two of the main aspects of art are invisible; the basic nature of art is invisible. The integrity of visual art is not seen. The unseen nature and integrity of art, the development of its aspects, the irreducibility of thought, can be replaced by falsifications, and by verbiage about the material, itself in reality unseen. The discussion of science is scientific; the discussion of art is superstitious. There is no history.

There has been some discussion of space, usually of proportion, by past architects, and some by historians of architecture. There is some by recent architects: practical by Alexander, practical and actual by Kahn, a little by van Doesburg, by Mies van der Rohe, by Le Corbusier, and by Wright. There is some in Japanese and Korean literature, mixed with an astrology of place, called *Pung-su* in Korean and *Feng-shui* in Chinese, both meaning "wind and water," classed vaguely in English as "geomancy". But the subject of space in architecture, the nature of architecture, is not developed. Judging from the evidence of the buildings by recent well-known architects, space in architecture is no longer known. It's not unseen; it's not there. Within the clothes there is no Emperor.

There has been almost no discussion of space in art, nor in the present. The most important and developed aspect of present art is unknown. This concern, my main concern, has no history. There is no context; there are no terms; there are not any theories. There is only the visible work invisible. Space is made by an artist or architect; it is not found and packaged. It is made by thought. Therefore most buildings have no space. Most people are not aware of this absence. They are not bothered by a confusion and a nothingness that is enclosed. Of course they don't miss real space and don't desire it. Sometimes when they are traveling they enter a cathedral, recognize space, and thank God instead of the architect. Some people recognize and want what they never knew existed. A few people have said to me, and one written, that my work together made space of a room, made architecture, and even that it made a "spiritual" space. Space is so unknown that the only comparison is to the beliefs of the past.

After a few thousand years space is so unknown that a discussion of it would have to begin with a rock. How large is it? Is it on a level surface? Does it rest on the surface or does it perch? If it isn't on a level surface, the tilted surface approaches a second entity. Is the rock symmetrical? If not, does it face away or toward the tilted surface? Is the top of the rock pointed, rounded, flat but symmetrical with the sides, flat but broader than the sides, so that the rock is a thick plane parallel to the surface, level or tilted? That is, in general, in what way does the rock create space around itself? It is a definition of space, a center of space, in one way a core of space. I'm not interested in skinny figures, but they are Giacometti's early and unusual creation of space. A related creation made earlier and by many architects is the scheme of the old Russian churches. The base, the church itself, is a hollow block, which is a form so far in advance of this discussion that I will never get to it. The top of the church, a single onion dome if the church is small, or one large dome and four smaller ones if the church is large, is like the pointed rock, but of course is definite, a core of space in the sky, developing from the solidly enclosed space below, contracting above the roof, swelling into a light volume and contracting to a point. The Kimbell Museum is like the rock on a tilted surface. It is at the foot of a long slope and instead of facing ahead in continuation of the slope, as is expected, it faces the slope, which becomes a secondary, half-defined space. In exception to the meager discussion of space Michael Benedikt describes the slope toward the Kimbell and relates it to geomancy.

Then, what if a second rock is placed nearby? I'm not describing how a primitive discussion of space began thousands of years ago, but how a primitive discussion might begin tomorrow, if this civilization were advanced enough to bear it. How far apart are the two rocks? Is one larger than the other? Two rocks of equal size and the space between them is a situation which is very different from that of a small rock and a large rock with the same space between. Do the rocks have the same shape or is one pointed and the other round? If they are on a slope, which is higher, which joins the plane as an entity?

If two objects are close together they define the space in between. These definitions are infinite until the two objects are so far apart that the distance in between is no longer space. But then the passerby remembers that one was there and another here. The space between can even be more definite than the two objects which establish it; it can be a single space more than the two objects are a pair. Of course I can't continue, I can't mention what would happen if a stick were put across the two stones. Over two hundred years ago Samuel Johnson kicked a rock to prove its existence; fifty years ago

Wallace Stevens described the effect of a jar upon the wilderness; this year there are two rocks; obviously this leisurely pace is too fast.

In this century, since the decline before its beginning of the traditional art of the diverse civilizations, within the subsequent art meant to be international, the development of space is only thirty years old. Until then an interest in space was not one of the main characteristics of international contemporary art. This was of course because the great change at the turn of the century occurred conservatively in painting. The contradictions of simulated space were primary. All sculpture, except for Giacometti's, before and including David Smith's – that of Rodin and Maillol and Brancusi and Arp, both of whose work I like better than Giacometti's – is traditional sculpture, which is primarily one rock with complications, or is low relief, one plane with complications. However, a new aspect begins in the work of Brancusi and Arp, which is that of the work as a whole. Art does not change in one line, not from A to B to C, but from V to 5 to L. But it does change; it has to change, unless science becomes immobilized into religion. I was not completely alone in the early '60s in developing space as a main aspect of art, but few artists were interested and then usually within an earlier context, the imagery in Bontecou's work and the remnants of Smith's, the standing position and the compositional elements, in Chamberlain's work. Later the interest in three-dimensionality and in space developed quickly, all kinds, a little, a lot. The most developed were the canvas works by Oldenburg, enclosing a soft space, a flexible space, and the glass works by Larry Bell, which contained a visible space, modified by a phenomenological aspect that has become an important new aspect, which Dan Flavin began somewhat earlier and Bob Irwin somewhat later. This aspect was begun by Pollock in his specific use of color and material. I think that I developed space as a main aspect of art. This aspect is now widespread at a low level, which wouldn't matter much if anyone mentioned that, and is the primary aspect in the work of the few very good younger artists, who, since space is invisible, are insufficiently recognized. Space is now a main aspect of present art, comparable only to color as a force. The other artist who has thoroughly developed space is of course Richard Serra.

The development of space is within the last thirty years. For one hundred years the most powerful aspect has been color. The one hundred years of the primacy of color is still only a beginning. Basically the present international art developed from the traditional representational art of Europe. The necessities of representation inhibited the use of color. An object is pale in the light and dark in the shade, allowing full color only in between, usually in smaller areas than the light and shade and usually well back from the frontal plane of the picture, to where the full color is subdued by aerial perspective. Chinese, Korean, and Japanese painting is also representational, but without the simulation of unified space, and is usually subdued to depict space. Japanese prints are an important exception to the attrition of color, as well as paintings on screens and the illustration of novels, all flat and bright. Goya said: "In art there is no need for color; I see only light and shade." The simulation of appearance, the depiction of objects in their space, upon a flat surface, a simulation of reality that must be believed by the viewer, is not compatible with a developed interest in color. The painting by Zeuxis that the birds pecked at could not have been like the painting on Attic vases, flat areas of red and black. It had to be a better version of the kind of depiction in the frescoes of Pompeii. The red and black of the vase painting is color; the color in the frescoes is an accompaniment. Romanesque painting, which has clear and strong and well organized areas of color, has always been safe from birds. I can imagine a Romanesque painter being horrified by Cimabue's modulation into representation of the areas of color. Since the painter represented the universe, he must have thought it decadent (at the beginning of the Renaissance) to represent an individual. The areas of color in Giotto's paintings are due to the past and are more important than the newly modeled faces, feet, and hands. Despite the high quality of the subsequent painting, color was a declining interest. But it is too particular and especially too important in organization to become minor, just secondary.

The discussion of space has been leisurely, like the exploration in Marvell's poem, or like the lawsuit over who owned the snow on Popocatépetl, which took two hundred years, while the knowledge of space which I've made grew swiftly. This is a great deal of knowledge, but not written, knowledge of a peculiar kind as visual art, made by a person, sometimes intelligible to other persons, not made by snakes or owls, probably not intelligible to intelligent beings elsewhere, perhaps not to our descendants in ten thousand years. The work is a great deal of knowledge about space, which is necessarily related to the space of architecture. This knowledge is, to me, particular and plentifully diverse; to almost everyone it doesn't exist; it's invisible.

I feel that I have the steam engine, but no tracks, or the gasoline engine, but no wheels. The Mexicans invented the wheel for toys but never thought to use the idea for transportation. Plenty of good ideas in so-called early civilizations were never developed. Civilizations, like art, do not change in a line: it's best to avoid the word "progress". Good ideas that were developed are now ignored in the industrial transition, such as the knowledge of space in traditional Korean and Japanese architecture or the knowledge of urban space in 18th-century European

Untitled, 1989, anodized aluminum, plexiglass, 6 units, each 9 7/8" x 19 5/8" x 9 7/8" (cat. no. 16)

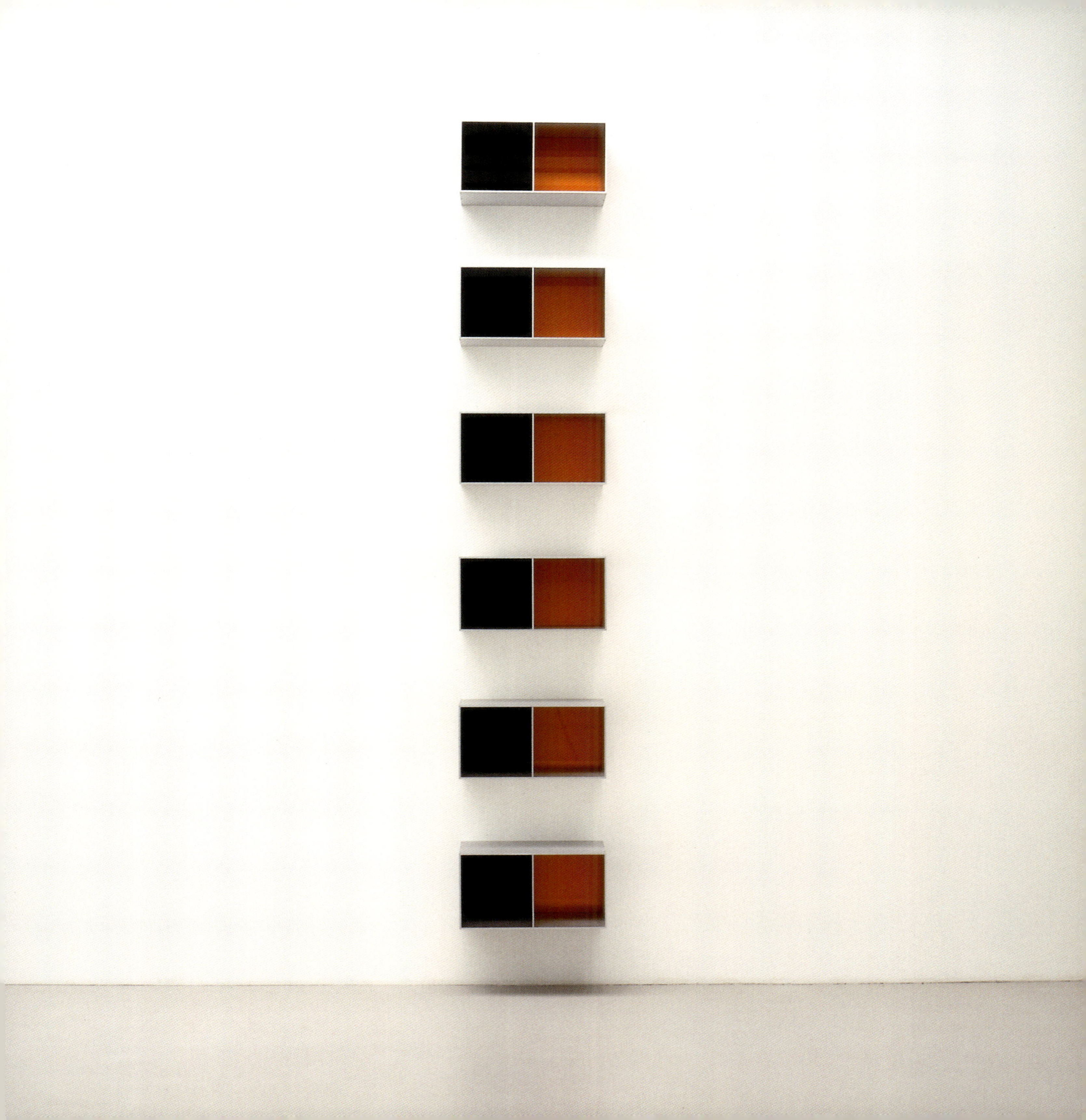

cities and 19th-century Paris. None of this quantity of knowledge, built, not written, is used in new construction. Seoul and Osaka are wastelands in which there are monuments and Paris is a curiosity surrounded by a desert. The earlier knowledge isn't regarded as knowledge, but as appearance, as style, and so cannot continue, cannot accumulate, as scientific knowledge does. There are books with plans about earlier architecture and cities but these plans are regarded as only history and not as relevant. There is no discussion of space in art and architecture in the present.

In 1962 I made a right angle of wood placed directly on the floor (ill. p. 6). This was preceded by another freely placed work and that by a work which I considered then to be high relief, but which I consider now to be the first three-dimensional work to be on the wall. For a long time it was on the floor. The size of the right angle is determined by the right angle of a black pipe, whose two open ends are the centers of the outer planes of the right angle, which is painted cadmium red light; red and black, and black as space. The right angle doesn't stand or sit and although it is vertical, 122 centimeters high, there is no way to believe it to be an abstracted figure, or an abstracted object. All sides are equal. There is scarcely an inside and an outside, only the space within the angle and the space beyond the angle. The only enclosed space is inside the pipe. This slight linear space determines the dimensions of the broad planes. The shell of this narrow space passes through the breadth of the inner angle, a definite space through a general space.

Before the right angle and its predecessor, all "sculpture" was placed on a pedestal or, finally, in David Smith's work, stood like a figure. Nothing had ever been placed directly on the floor. As I've written before, I think there was a small flat work on the floor by Lucas Samaras done at the same time or earlier. Since now it is common for work to be placed anywhere in a room, it is impossible for people to understand that placement on the floor and the absence of a pedestal were inventions. I invented them. But there is no history.

One of the many destructive assumptions now is that all ideas have no originators; they are mutations in the public domain. The use and meaning of the ideas are vague. But someone invents ideas. Someone wants something new. In its invention an idea is clear and in its diffusion it is vague. This is easy to see. It's easy to see that Chamberlain invented Stella's reliefs. A new idea is quickly debased, often before the originator has time and money to continue it. In general I think this has happened to all of my work, but especially to the use of the whole room, which is now called an installation, which basically I began. Oldenburg's *Store* was a store but it could be called an installation. Bob Whitman's performances occured in installations. Several years later Yayoi Kusama made a free-standing room and Lucas Samaras also. In 1967 in Los Angeles a work of Carl Andre's, *8 Cuts*,

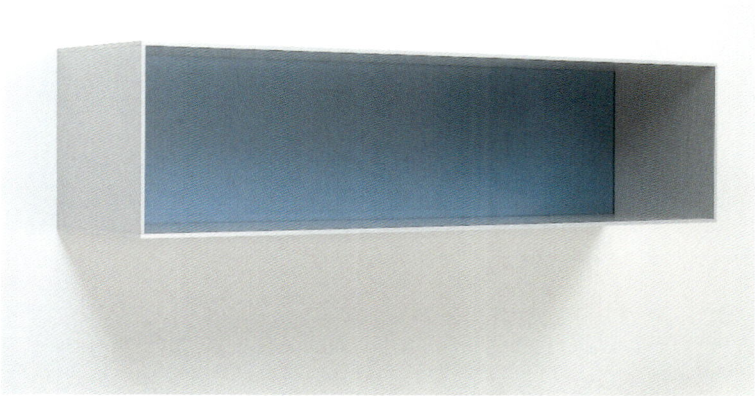

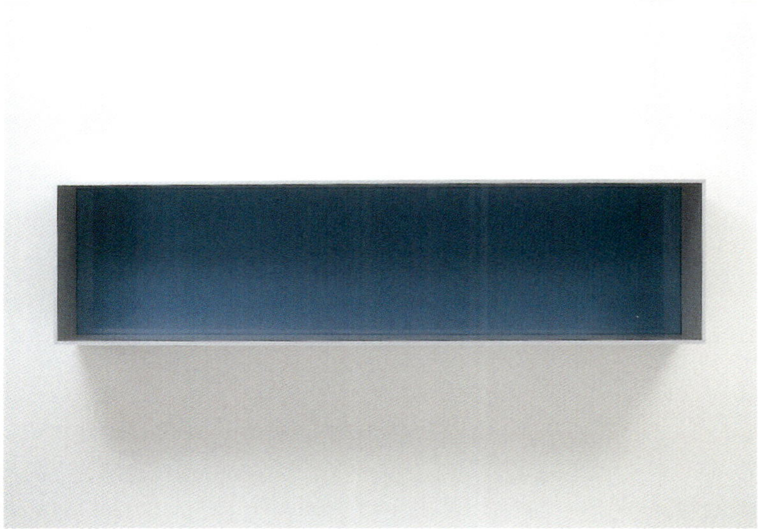

Untitled, 1988, aluminum, plexiglass, 9 7/8“ x 39 3/4“ x 9 7/8“ (cat. no. 12)

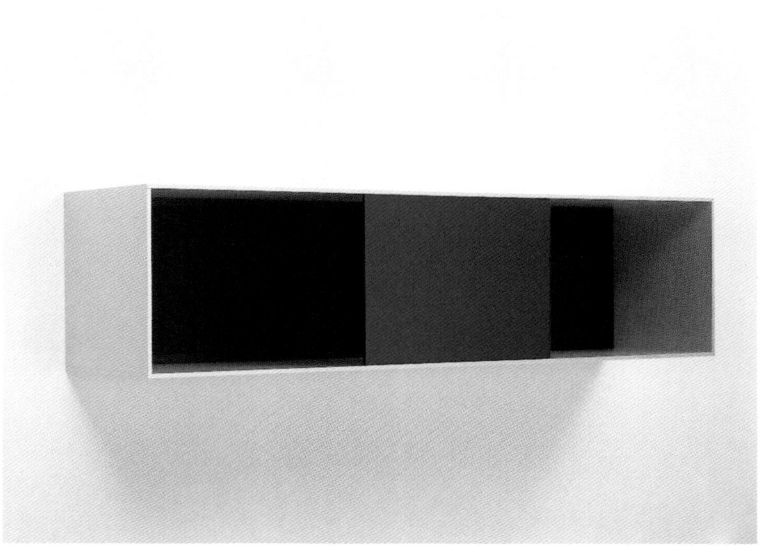

Untitled, 1991, aluminum, anodized aluminum, transparent blue over red plexiglass, 9 7/8" x 39 3/4" x 9 7/8" (cat. no. 24)

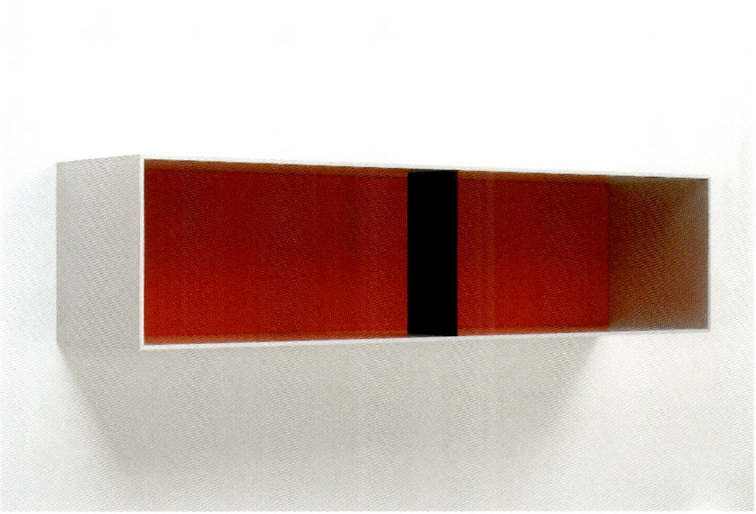

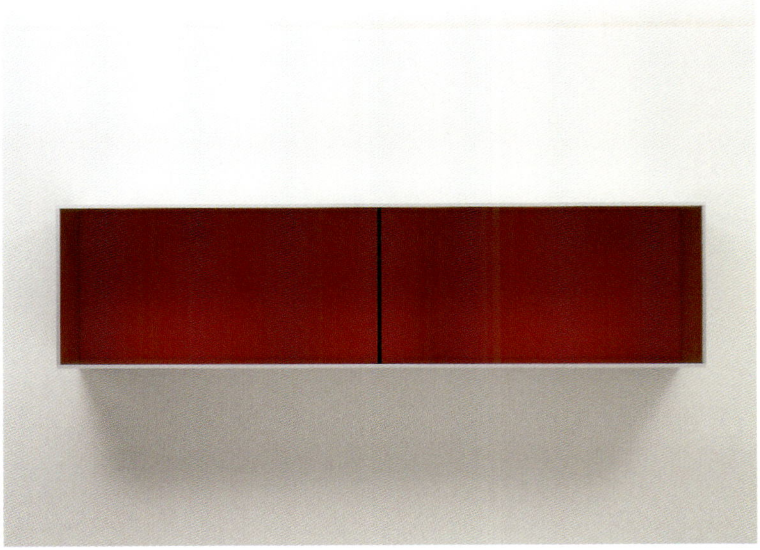

Untitled, 1991, aluminum, anodized aluminum, plexiglass, 9 7/8“ x 39 3/4“ x 9 7/8“ (cat. no. 22)

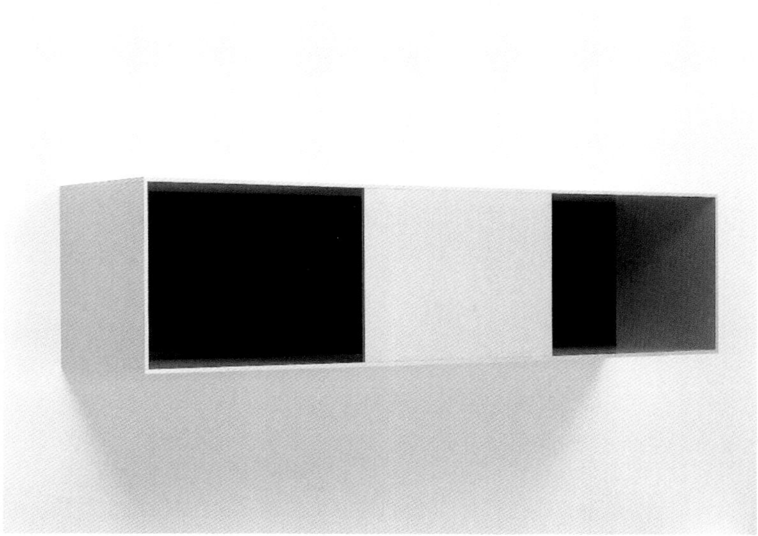

Untitled, 1991, aluminum, transparent yellow over black plexiglass, 9 7/8" x 39 3/4" x 9 7/8" (cat. no. 25)

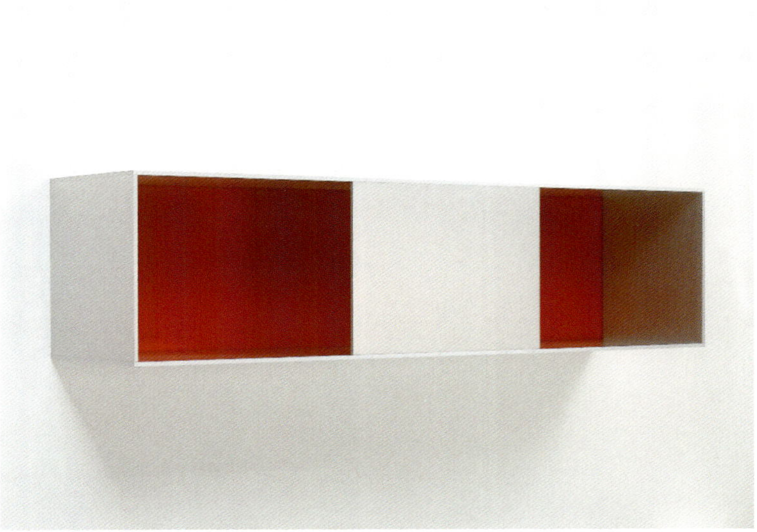

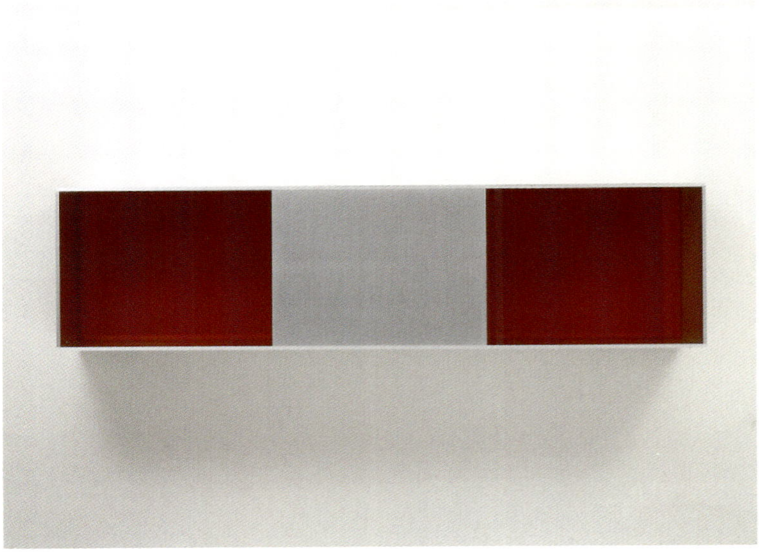

Untitled, 1991, aluminum, transparent yellow over red plexiglass, 9 7/8" x 39 3/4" x 9 7/8" (cat. no. 23)

covered the floor of the gallery. Of course in 1923 Lissitzky built the *Proun Raum* and in the late '20s Schwitters built the *Merzbau*. One work occupying a whole room is still alive and new in the work of a few artists – Roni Horn, Michael Schulz, Ilya Kabakov – but many artists degrade the idea, for example Barbara Kruger, who is my favorite, because she also degrades red and black. Again there is no discussion and criticism of works that occupy rooms, which is a reason why it is possible to have bland and trite work, with one or two meager and obvious ideas spread over a whole room, usually in writing, without space, which is after all the origin of the form.

My work with the whole room began with part of it. In 1965 I made a work that extended from the floor to the ceiling. This extended the definite space between the units to those below and above. In 1966 I made six galvanized-iron units which extended from wall to wall, so that the corners became definite and the whole end of the room articulated. In 1969 there was an anodized aluminum work, now destroyed, which was on the floor and against the wall, also wall to wall. And in the same year a work made of coldrolled steel, now destroyed, with 11 units that extended from corner to corner the length of the room. Also in that year I made a work of many galvanized iron units which occupied about a third of an otherwise empty room, a work in relation to the whole room. This is now in Texas. In 1970 I made what is usually described as a galvanized iron wall which went around three sides of a room. This is a whole room. It's in Texas. In Portland in 1974 we built a very large voluminous plywood work around three sides of the space.

In 1960 very little that was traditionally three-dimensional was placed on the wall, only the low reliefs by Arp, which are better than usually thought. None of the large reliefs by Schwitters were in New York City. Later, Oldenburg made low reliefs of plaster for his *Store* and later Bontecou made high reliefs and later again Chamberlain made high reliefs. No one is interested in this sequence of development, as no one is interested in the development of a whole room as one work. Art historians of the past are at least interested in chronology. Art historians of the present are not. It's too real and interferes with treating the present as the past, but with less substance, a subject of their speculation.

Low and high relief are basically painting, possessing the same problems, as well as some of their own. After I made the first works placed on the floor, knowing the new relationship to a surface, through at least 1963 I didn't think anything could be made which could be placed on the wall. Then I realized that the relationship to the wall could be the same as that to the floor. The work on the floor was not lying flat upon it, therefore it was not low relief on the floor, nor heaped upon it, therefore it was not high relief on the floor. This discussion seems long but it's brief. Most relationships and exceptions can't be mentioned, but one exception is that I don't consider Carl Andre's works on the floor to be low relief, regardless of being flat. My work on the floor was a new form, creating space amply and strongly. The relationship could be the same to the wall. It was necessary for the work to project sufficiently, at least as much as its height and width. I never made this minimum, which would be a cube.

The first such work, in 1964, was horizontal, made of leftover plywood semicircles, and it projected further than its height. The same year a small work that projects was constructed by a nearby factory. In 1965, the factory made, then and now a condemnation to hell, a vertical work of ten units, each short in relation to the depth, all together long, and, as I said, with spaces equal to those between the units at the floor and at the ceiling, with luck. The necessary difference was that the work not be flattened, low or high, to the wall, whether it be small or large. This invention is still not understood, or rather it is completely lost. Derivations are everywhere, but are always low or high relief, new in appearance only. The small- and medium-sized works on the wall have been those in which it has been most possible to develop color.

The discussion of color is greater than the discussion of space, and unlike the missing particularities of space, it describes to redundancy the particularities of color. Primarily this has been because with the creation of science in the 17th century the study of color has been part of science. And like astronomy it has been cursed with its own astrology. The discussion of color has not been leisurely, like that of space. Instead of millennia, the speed has been in generations. There is a history of color, first in philosophy and then in science. Aristotle said that there was in the category of substance an entity that might have an aspect of the category of quality: material was primary, color was secondary. He said, to quote Copleston, that "matter is at once the principle of individuation and unknowable in itself." There is a history of color in art. Every other generation has a new idea of color. However, this is a generation without ideas. At the present space and color have in common complete neglect. Despite the primary importance of color for more than a hundred years there are now no theories. The last philosophy of color, which is what it was, as well as being factual, and the mixture may be unavoidable, at least in art, was that of Josef Albers in *The Interaction of Color* of 1963. In Part I, Albers begins:

If one says "Red" (the name of a color) and there are 50 people listening, it can be expected that there will be 50 reds in their minds. And one can be sure that all these reds will be very different.

That is a philosophy and it does not agree with what Albers was taught in the Bauhaus.

I knew as a child that certain colors were supposed to produce certain feelings. I didn't understand why a bull should be mad at red. Johannes Itten and Kandinsky taught in their important color courses at the Bauhaus that colors always produce the same emotions, and also the colors always correspond to certain shapes, the two together agreeing on the emotion. The idea that I like best is Kandinsky's that a pentagon combines a square, which is red, with triangles, which are yellow, to make orange. The idea should be sent to Washington so that the newly painted Pentagon could be the first to use color in war. The square is death; the triangle is vehemence. The circle is blue and is infinite and peaceful. As with God and patriotism, I didn't take the attributions of color seriously enough to contemplate. I don't remember such ideas being discussed in the '50s or after. In contrast, the terms "warm" and "cool" are still used as description, but also as thermometers of feeling. The more vague an idea, the longer it lasts; in decay it becomes even more vague and lasting.

A basic problem for an artist at the beginning is that while color is crucial in their work, its development being a force, the information about color is extensive and occurs in many forms, partly technical and partly philosophical. The technical information is irrelevant and uninteresting until it is needed. The philosophy seldom fits. There is a limit to how much an artist can learn in advance. An artist works only step to step into the unknown while the particular knowledge of color exists and is vast; the particulars of the world are infinite. This is overwhelming in an urgent situation. Color is very hard to learn, since it is hard to know what is useful. The particulars must be the artist's own. Nevertheless, color should be taught to the beginning artist, first, as knowledge which may be relevant, second, as knowledge of the history of art, which is the history of the activity and of the history of color in that activity, and third, as day-to-day new knowledge for the new artist, who should only be taught from the beginning as an artist. That help should be step by step as it is needed in a completely individual effort. This sounds obvious but few understand how much of a process it is to make art. It is very much building, as I said, step by step. These remarks about art education seem innocuous but they imply a revolution. For example, no one but a daily, actual, working artist of some worldly standing, as things are now, should teach art. Otherwise it's like a non-plumber teaching plumbing. No one but someone who is beginning as an artist should be taught. Why learn to plumb, of you're not going to?

Artists cannot teach the history of their activity. They seldom can teach the activity of their own activity. They have no connections with those interested in art and with the public. They cannot explain their activity. This is part of what is wrong. This is partly why the integrity of art is steadily less. There cannot be an education of artists that is distant, distorted, and institutionalized with the expectation that in five or ten years a good artist will result. The result is another institutionalized new teacher.

The last real picture of real objects in a real world was painted by Courbet. After that no one was so sure about the real world, so

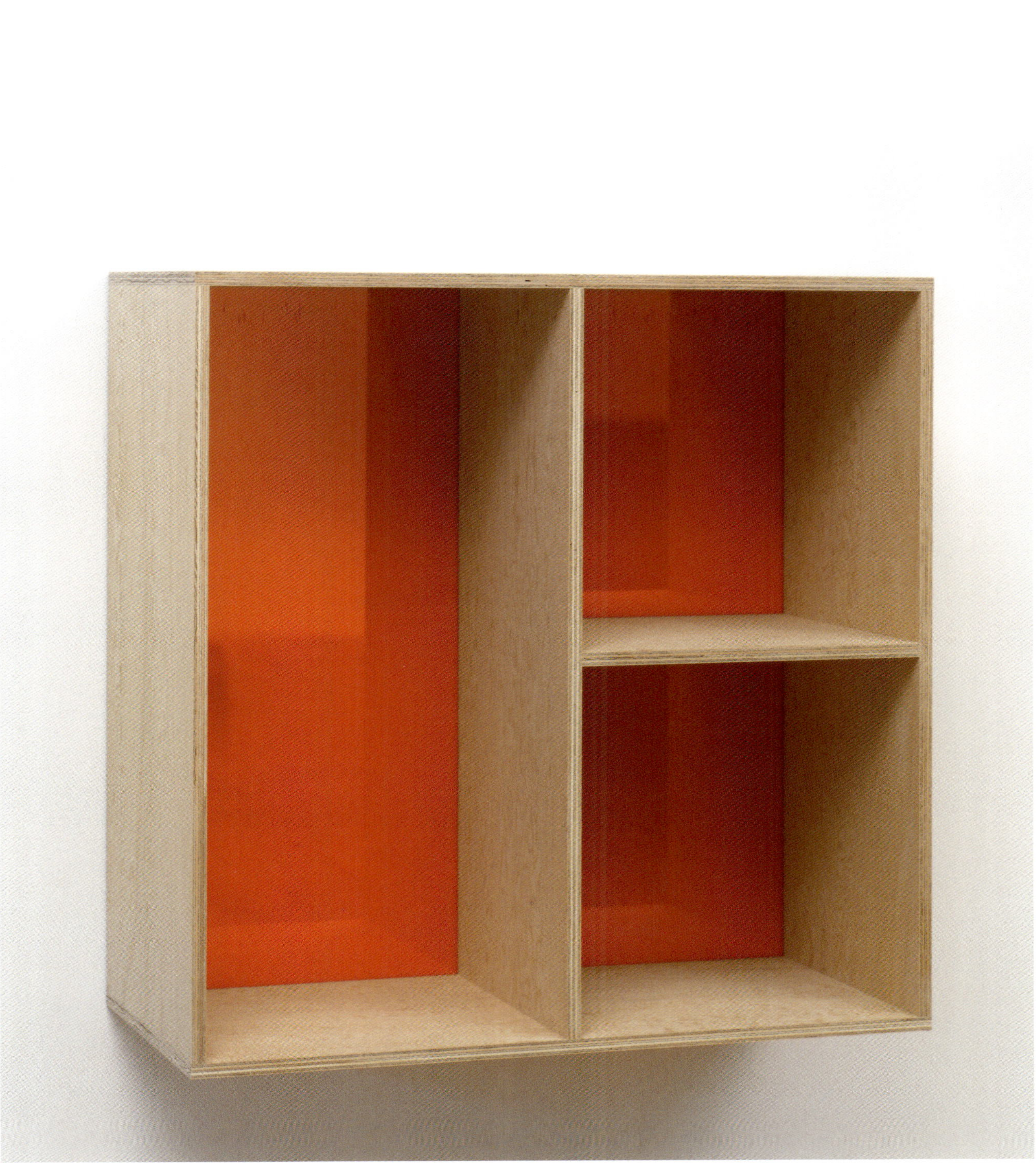

Untitled, 1986, Douglas Fir plywood, plexiglass, 39 3/4" x 39 3/4" x 19 5/8"

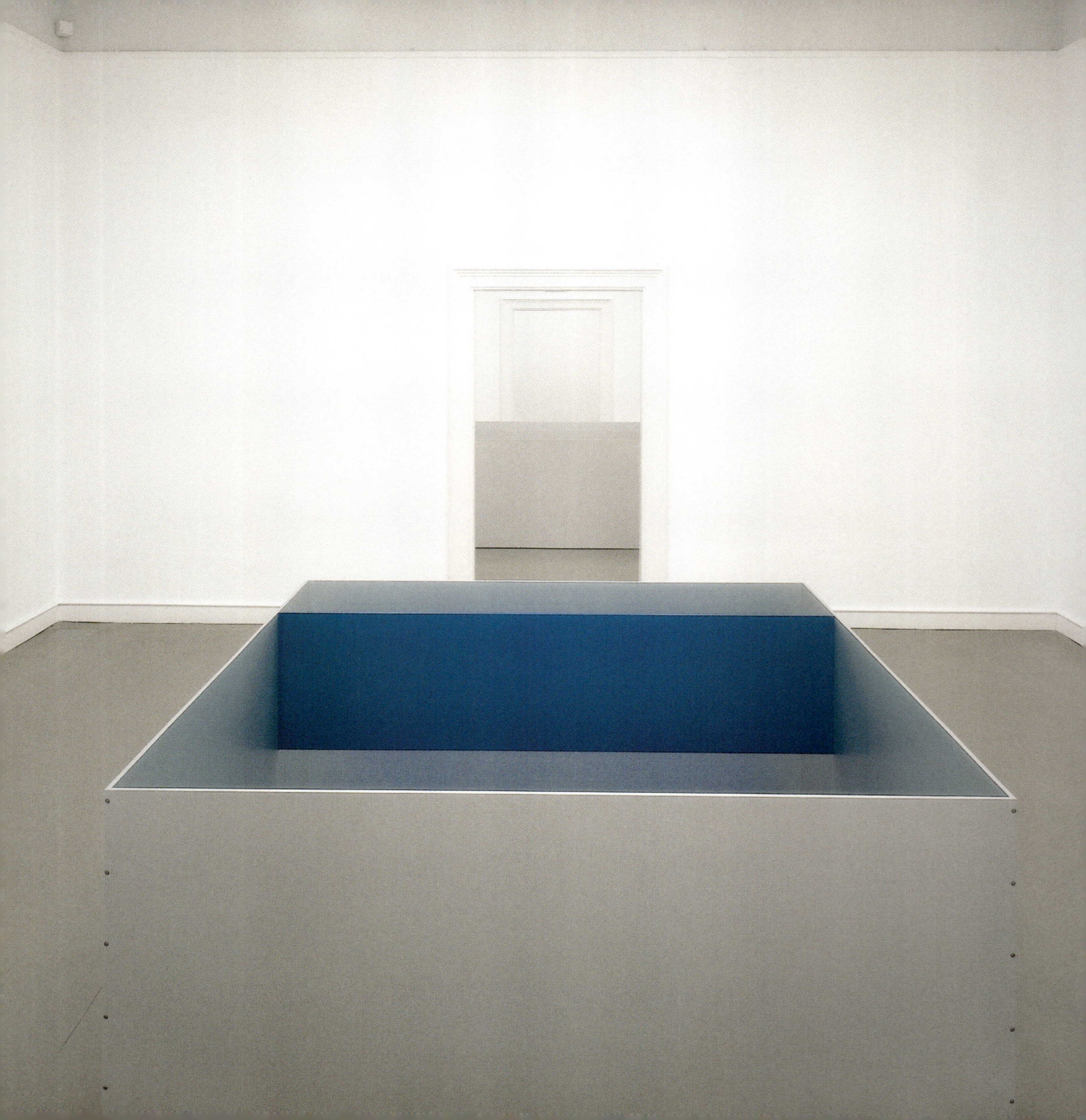

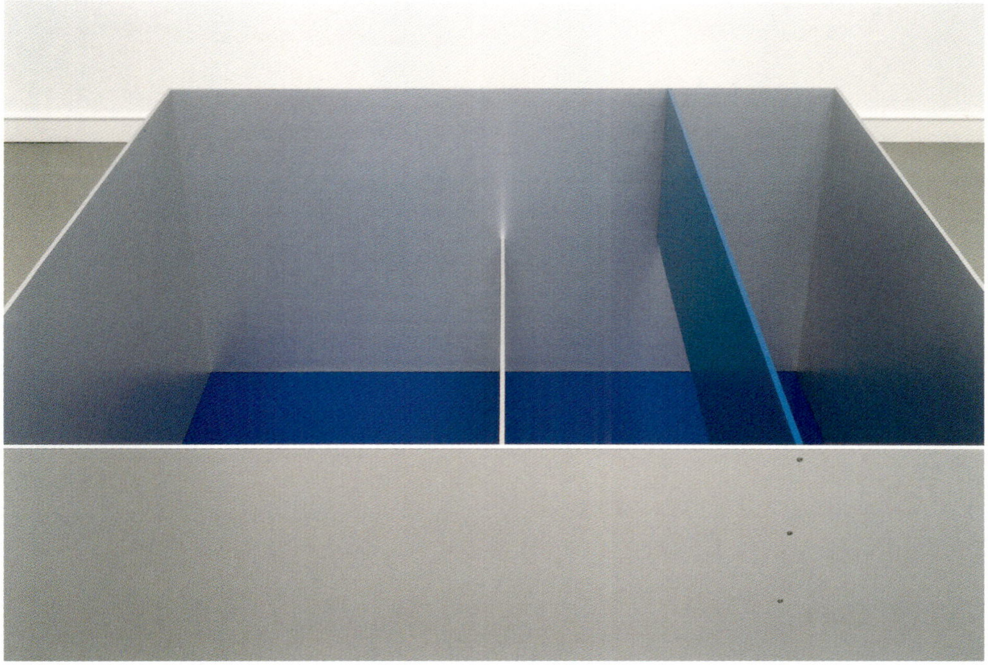

Untitled, 1989, anodized aluminum, plexiglass, 39 3/4" x 79 1/2" x 39 3/4" (cat. no. 18)

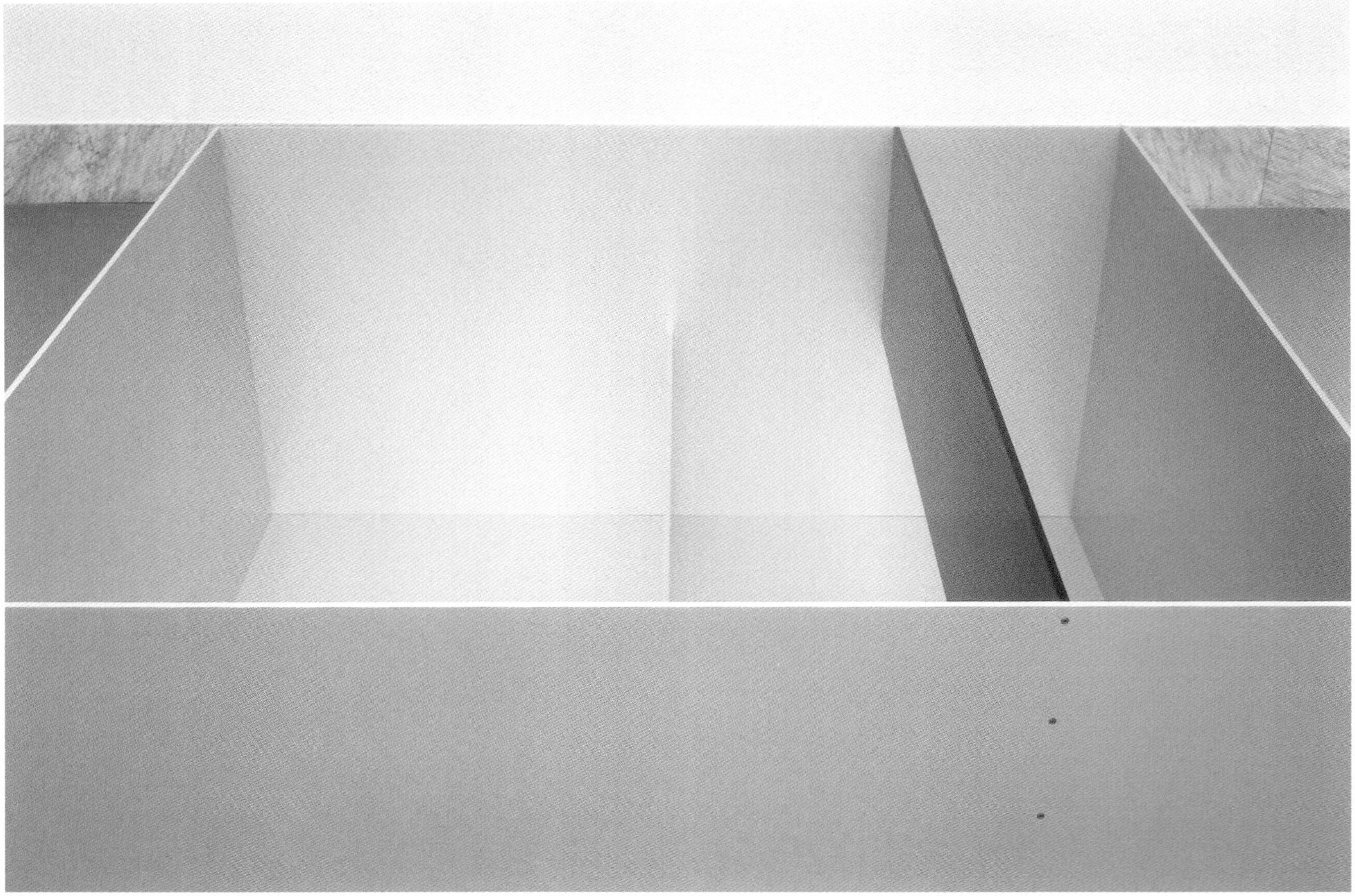

Untitled, 1989, anodized aluminum, 39 3/4" x 79 1/2" x 39 3/4" (cat. no. 19)

Untitled, 1989, anodized aluminum, 39 3/4" x 79 1/2" x 39 3/4" (cat. no. 19)

that when it came to keeping a color or an undescriptive shape at the cost of accurate representation, the latter lost. From Manet onward the concerns of painting itself developed quickly. This is the conventional history of recent painting. Nothing like this happened in sculpture, since being in space there was no conflict, and there was no color. It was conservative and was not bothered by the problem of how the world is known. The trouble and cost of its making had to have been a factor. The history of the increasing emphasis on the means of painting is very large and detailed. More than the so-called form, or the shapes, color is the most powerful force. In retrospect, and only so, the expansion of color is logical until the 1960s, concluding with the painting of Pollock, Newman, Still, and Rothko. The need for color, the meaning of that need, more than anything, destroyed the earlier representational painting, whether in Europe or Asia. In the work of all of the wellknown painters, color is amplified beyond anything seen for centuries, even in the work of Munch, whose work is not considered abstract. In the work of most – Matisse, Mondrian, Malevich, Léger, the four just mentioned – color is the dominant aspect, as black and white photographs show. Color is an immediate sensation, a phenomenon, and in that leads to the work of Flavin, Bell, and Irwin.

All experience is knowledge: subjective experience is knowledge; objective experience, which is science, is obviously knowledge. Color is knowledge. As Albers says, it is very subjective, even hard to remember. Color is also objective. In Part VIII Albers says to paste a red circle and a white circle on a black sheet of paper and then stare at the red circle. Then, look at the white circle: it is green or blue-green, the complementary of red. Allowing for everything human being subjective, this is absolutely objective. Color as knowledge is very durable. I find it difficult, maybe impossible, to forget. A considerable effort in the painted sheet, aluminum work that I made was to forget the colors and their combinations that I had liked and used in my first paintings, those in turn sometimes derived from Mondrian, Léger, or Matisse, or earlier European painters. Newman of course faced this definition and durability when he painted the three paintings he called *Who's Afraid of Red, Yellow and Blue*. He didn't go so far as to challenge red, yellow, blue, and white. Mondrian's colors are one of the facts and wonders of the world; there aren't seven anymore. Perhaps if the four colors were equal in extent they would not longer belong to Mondrian. The preponderance of white to the bright colors is of course the determining ratio.

It's a shame to provide arguments in support of museums, but in 1947 I lived in Philadelphia where there is one. In it there is the left panel, the crucifixion, by Roger van der Weyden. The colors I remember are blue, not soft, and red, high and slightly rosy. In my present vocabulary they are similar to RAL-Farben 3027, *Himbeerrot*, and RAL-5013, *Kobaltblau*. In art school I used them in a little painting and they remained van der Weyden's.

I painted over them. I don't know where I saw, perhaps only in books, Gerard David's light gray and cobalt blue, which is not 5013. Giorgione's and Titan's deep blue and orange brown is vast and inescapable. El Greco is interesting of course because he was from Crete, from which Theophanes earlier went to Russia, and so because of the influence of the Romanesque use of color in large areas. El Greco's colors are of one type, often glazed, and match where nothing is suspected to exist: alizarin crimson, viridian, a clear yellow and ultramarine blue. Except for the yellow these are all dark, but they are all clear, like stained glass. The Philadelphia Museum of Art also has many paintings by Mondrian. The first museum that I loved for art and hated for architecture was the Nelson Gallery and Atkins Museum in Kansas City, which has one of the best collections of Chinese art. The gray-green celadon from Korea is another durable color, of course a glaze, which is another important aspect. Also virtually glazed, but by oil, is the brown-black of the trees and the high green-blue of the sky in Ralph Blakelock's paintings.

Color in architecture began and ended with De Stijl. Earlier and later it is decoration or it is the usually quiet colors of materials. The colors of the bronze and the tinted glass of the building by Mies van der Rohe in New York City form as definite a scheme as any with bright colors. The question is whether architecture should always be quiet, with natural materials, usually gray or tan, or whether it should always be brightly colored or partly colored. In the present noisy and cluttered society, urban and rural, the obvious recommendation is to avoid color. As seen in bright signs everywhere, color becomes further junk. But without color, which is almost always on signs, most cities are junk anyway, the newest the worst.

Within De Stijl, van Doesburg was by far the most interested in color in architecture. He wanted a new activity, that of "colorist", to apply to architecture, which was always more conservative, as in the "collaboration", as van Doesburg conceived it between himself and J. J. P. Oud in De Vonk in 1917 and '18 and with Jan Wils in De Lange in 1917. But Oud said that van Doesburg was not being practical, which meant that the neighbors would be offended. Van Doesburg designed the interior of the Café Aubette in Strasbourg form 1926 to '28 within what he now considered a "collective" with Jean Arp, Sophie Taeuber-Arp, and Paul Horn as architect, but the owners modified it to the public's complaints within two years. Basically van Doesburg was applying planes of color, at an angle, which he thought harmonious and dynamic, to the orthogonal structure of the architecture, which he thought ordinary. Aside from the ever discouraging public, this division could not continue. Color has to be part of the usually right-angular architecture. So far this has not been done. The use of color by Rietveld is very nice but does not exceed decoration by much. The work of Luis Baragan is a possibility but I haven't seen it and the photographs are more pretty than informative. Van Doesburg thought of the painted window frames of De Lange as planes of color moving across the facade. He was wishful, but this and others are still good ideas.

Mondrian, Malevich, van Doesburg, and others made or tried to make art and architecture as part of a new civilization, which obviously it was, and obviously still is. They are generally disparaged as being idealistic and utopian, Mondrian's philosophy aside. Why is it idealistic – even what does that mean – to want to do something new and beneficial, practical also, in a new civilization? Is it practical to let the civilization become as gross as it is becoming, to let it become stagnant, and then in a few hundred years try to aerate it? By then it will completely inert, so that nothing can be done and nothing even imagined to be done. No one will realize that there isn't civilization. As usual the civilization will be convinced of not being one by its collapse. Why should everything be commercial? Just existing, even well, is not supposed to be civilized. And again, what does commercial mean? That has a wide range. As I mentioned, Oud argued to van Doesburg that he was being practical, that he was building what could be built in the circumstances, part of which were the neighbors. This is not practical, but conventional. The judgment of the neighbors is based upon meager knowledge and is determined by their narrow time and place and especially by their idea of status in the society, part of the narrowness, which is the greatest myth of this time. Anyway, the ignorance of the neighbors has a wide range, from that of the few rich to the not as rich to what is now called the middle class in the United States, but is lower, to those who know only a thousand words and can't read, again in the United States. Should art and architecture be made for a class or for each class? The neighbors have formed a taste among themselves, strangely worldwide, which is exploited by business. A town nearby in West Texas, which has a well-restored fort, is visited by tourists, who sometimes remain. These are all of a class and they slowly remake the town into what their scanty and sentimental knowledge makes them think a town of the Old West should look like. Should they be encouraged? If the knowledge of artists and architects is discredited, and of science, and only the very slowly growing knowledge of the great mass, if it grows, narrow class by class, is to be acted upon, then it will be hundreds of years before a real civilization develops, if ever, because commerce, in accordance with the neighbors' taste, will have designed everything in the world and the people as well. Clinton said recently, "You have to change the behavior of the whole country. People have to change their lives."

Frank Lloyd Wright wrote that a house with a view should be built below the top of a hill, not on the top, out of the wind, primarily to be unobtrusive in the landscape. The same advice applies to color. In new and empty land, in well-cultivated land, as in Tuscany, and even in suburban land approaching visual mis-

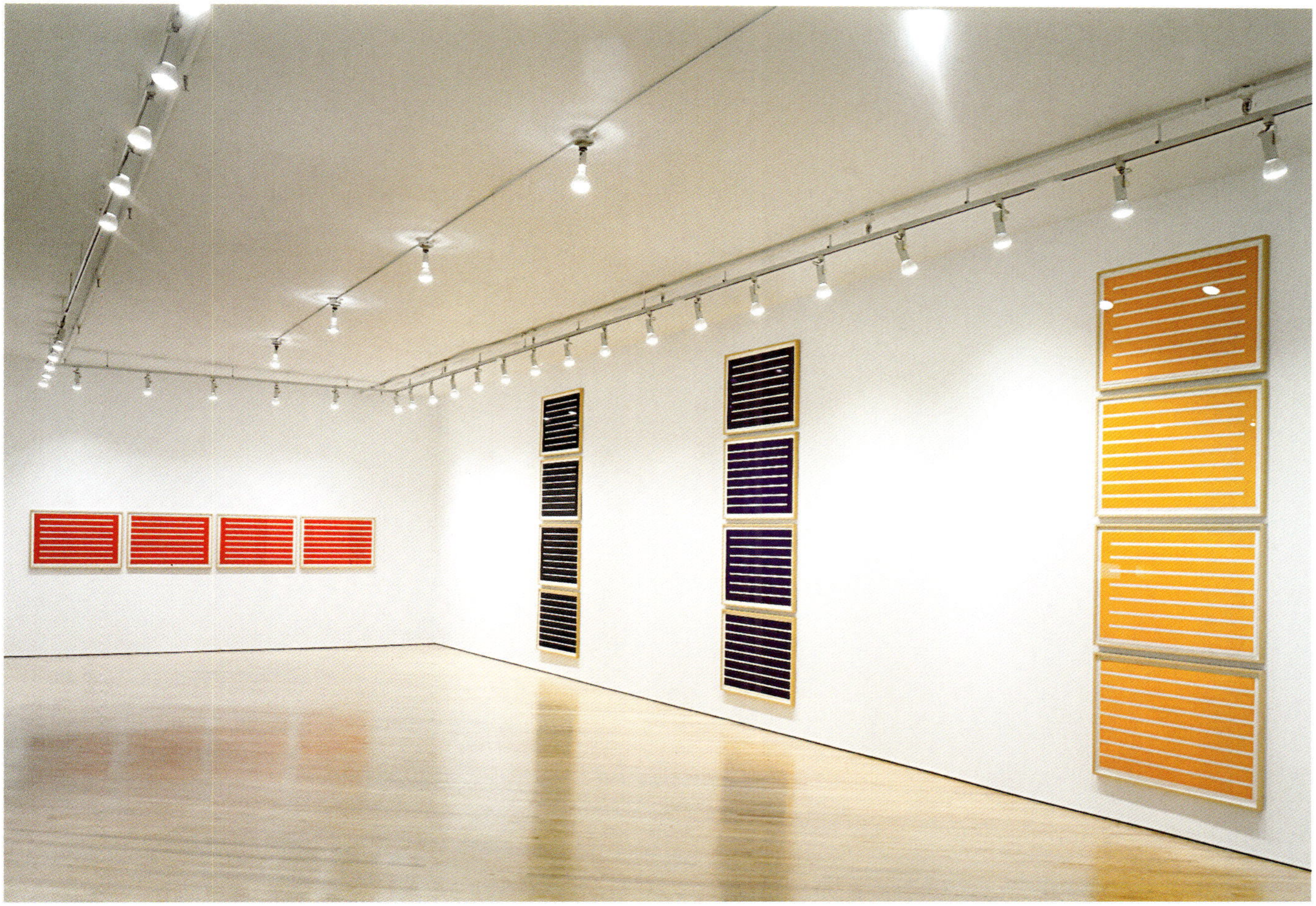

Installation, Brooke Alexander Editions, New York 1994

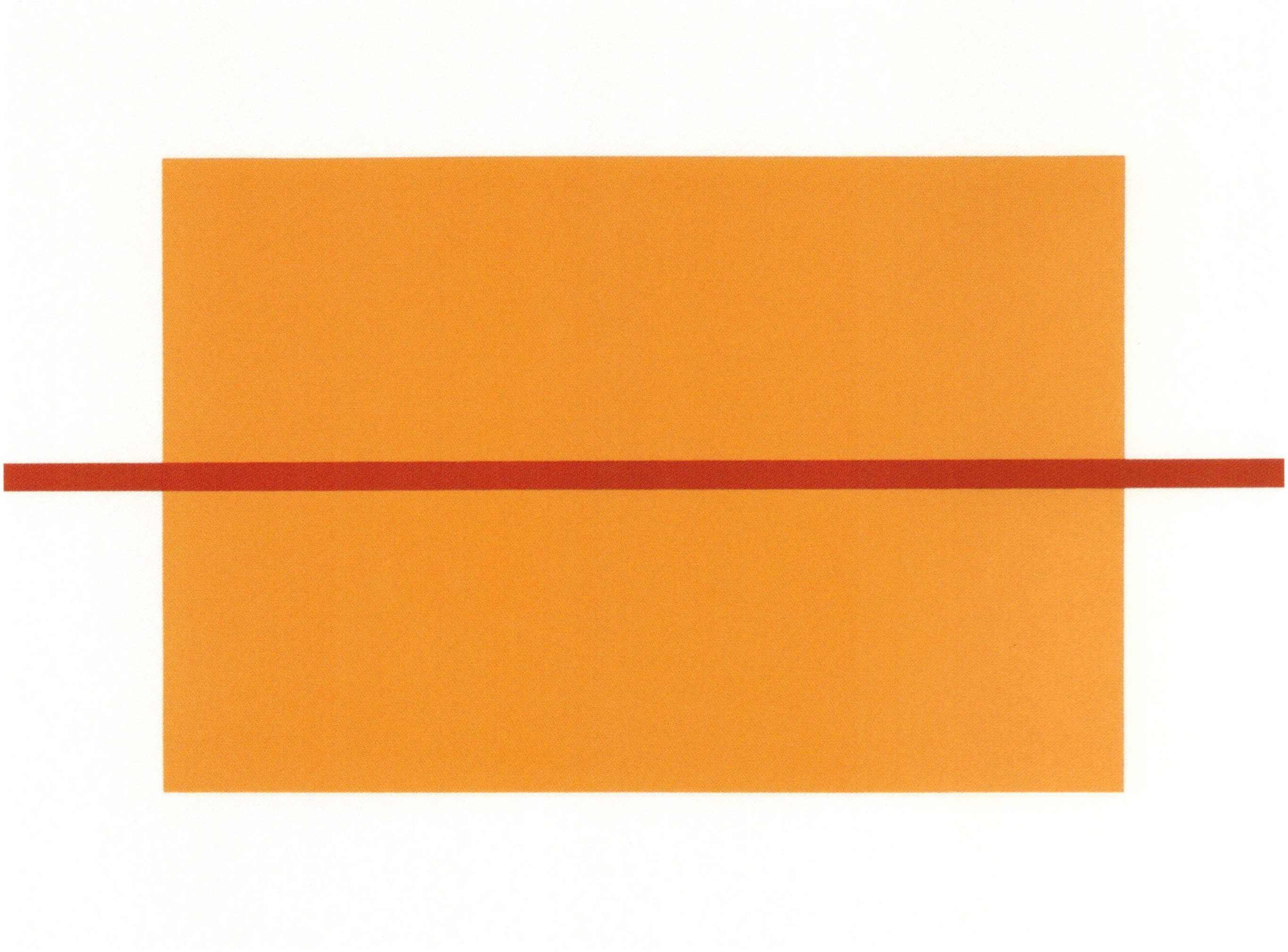

Ill. pp. 102–105: **Untitled, 1990, set of 7 woodcuts, each 23 1/2" x 31 1/2" (paper size) (cat. nos. 48–54)**

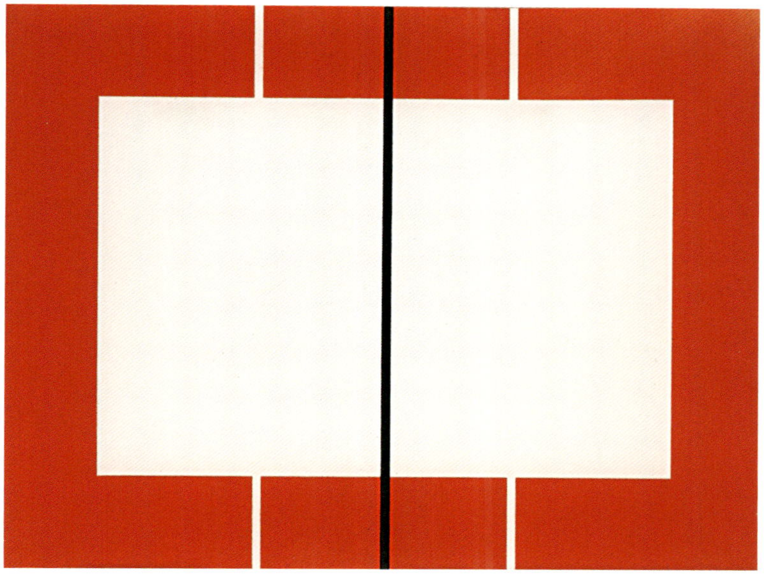

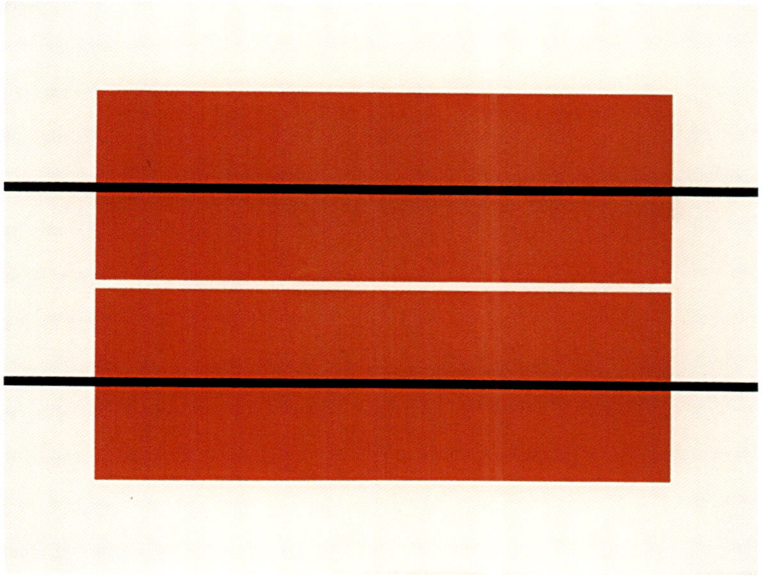

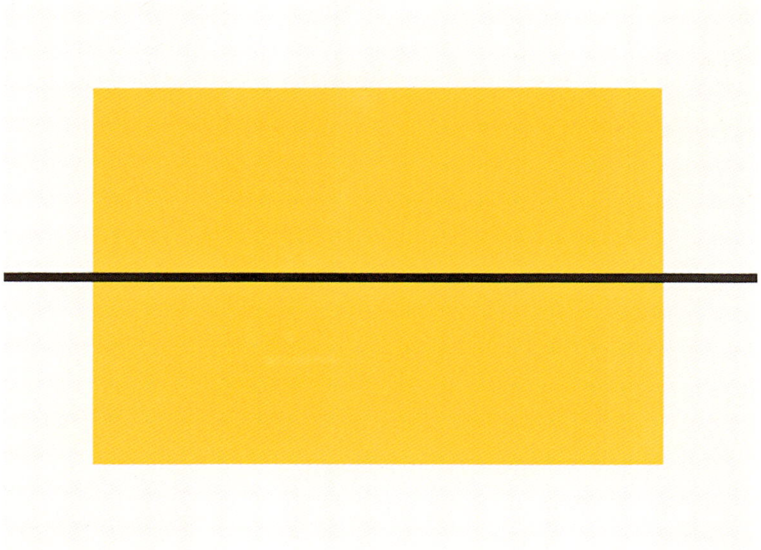

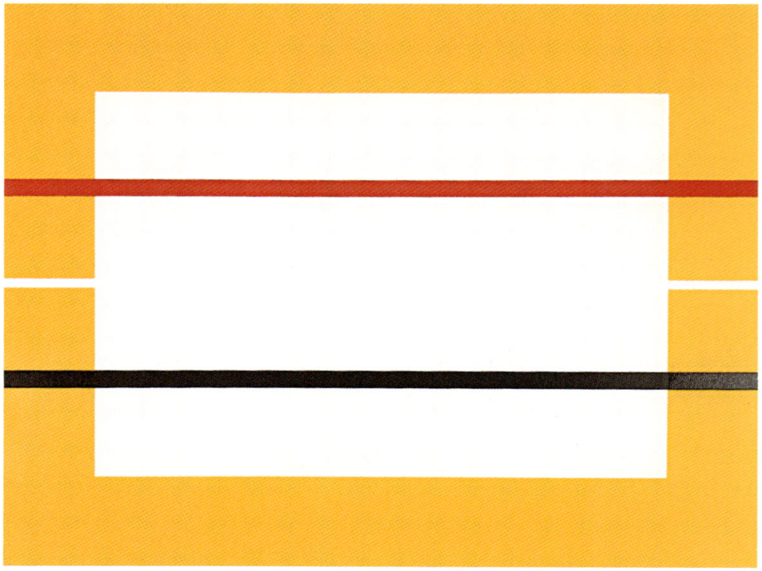

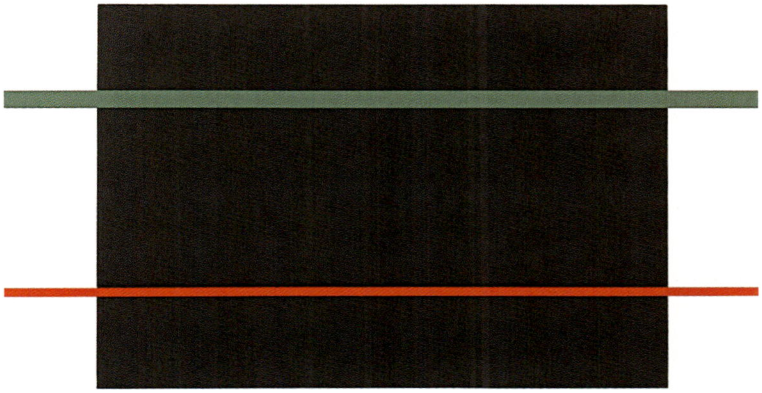

ery, it is wrong to construct obtrusive buildings. Whether they are obtrusive or not depends on the presence or absence of trees and on whether the land is flat or high. A bright building in the desert seems a mistake. In the polders perhaps not. The best argument for brightly colored buildings are those of St. Petersburg and Pushkin or Tsarskoe Selo, pink or turquoise. The white of the old churches in Russia is conspicuous in summer, like the large white rabbits without snow which I once saw in January in the archipelago off Stockholm, and then the churches are evanescent in winter. The color is not disagreeable partly because it is on isolated buildings and partly because it occurs on flat land among trees or among yellow and tan buildings, where it cannot be seen from far away, except for the Winter Palace. The buildings of the city of St. Petersburg improve the land, which is seldom the case. In Tuscany, the cultivation improves the land, which is also rare. The yellow ochre and red ochre of the buildings fits very well and the land even tolerates castles on the hilltops. In Korea an old village is beautiful, with thatched roofs, or with black tiles on the roofs, and with tiles on the adobe walls, lying quietly in the land, looking like the land. In both Korea and Japan the tiles on the roof are often red or blue plastic. In Japan the traditional high thatched roof is often replaced by the same shape in colored metal, including the old crosspieces at the ends of the peak.

In general, bright color adds to the bedlam. But then, just as the continuous noise in some cities, especially New York, is thoughtless, so is the use of color and materials. It's usual for a building to have half a dozen materials on the facade or in the lobby, which is as excruciating as the garbage truck beeping backwards and grinding. What if someone thought about the color of a building or of the colors of a town or city as a whole? But the answer to this question will not arrive. There is no sign of real color in present architecture, most of it called "post-Modern," in which, if there is a little more color, it is small decoration become larger. Color is misused in this architecture, as is its more or less prefabricated construction, the source of the style.

Many cities are built within a few years, or areas of cities are built that are so huge as to be cities themselves, usually built brutally in regard to the land. In Hong Kong not just a hillside is bulldozed, as in Los Angeles, it's the whole hill that is remade. The scale of everything in East Asia is greater; it's what New York must have seemed like in the '20s. Of course the buildings are mindlessly repetitive, relieved by kitsch when there is money. Along the southern shore of the Han River in Seoul there must be a hundred huge slabs of apartment buildings, identical, numbered, probably because it seems exotic, in huge Arabic numbers. The dwellers must like this. I think it's hell. They can't desire diversity. But this is one of the most important and difficult problems in architecture and urban planning. Diversity was created in small projects in the '20s and '30s, for example that by

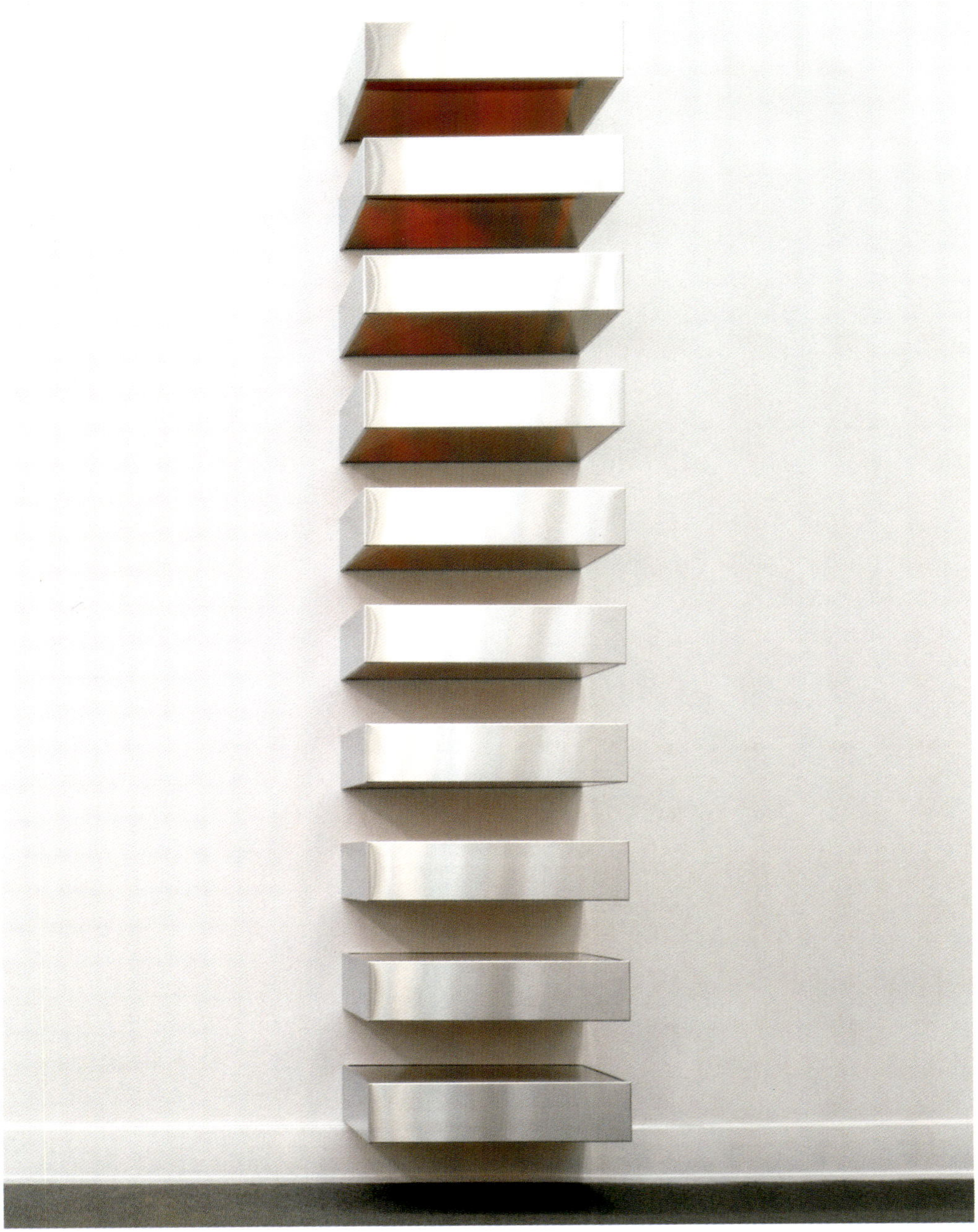

Untitled, 1990, stainless steel, plexiglass, 10 units, each 9 $^{7}/_{8}$" x 39 $^{3}/_{4}$" x 30 $^{1}/_{2}$" (cat. no. 20)

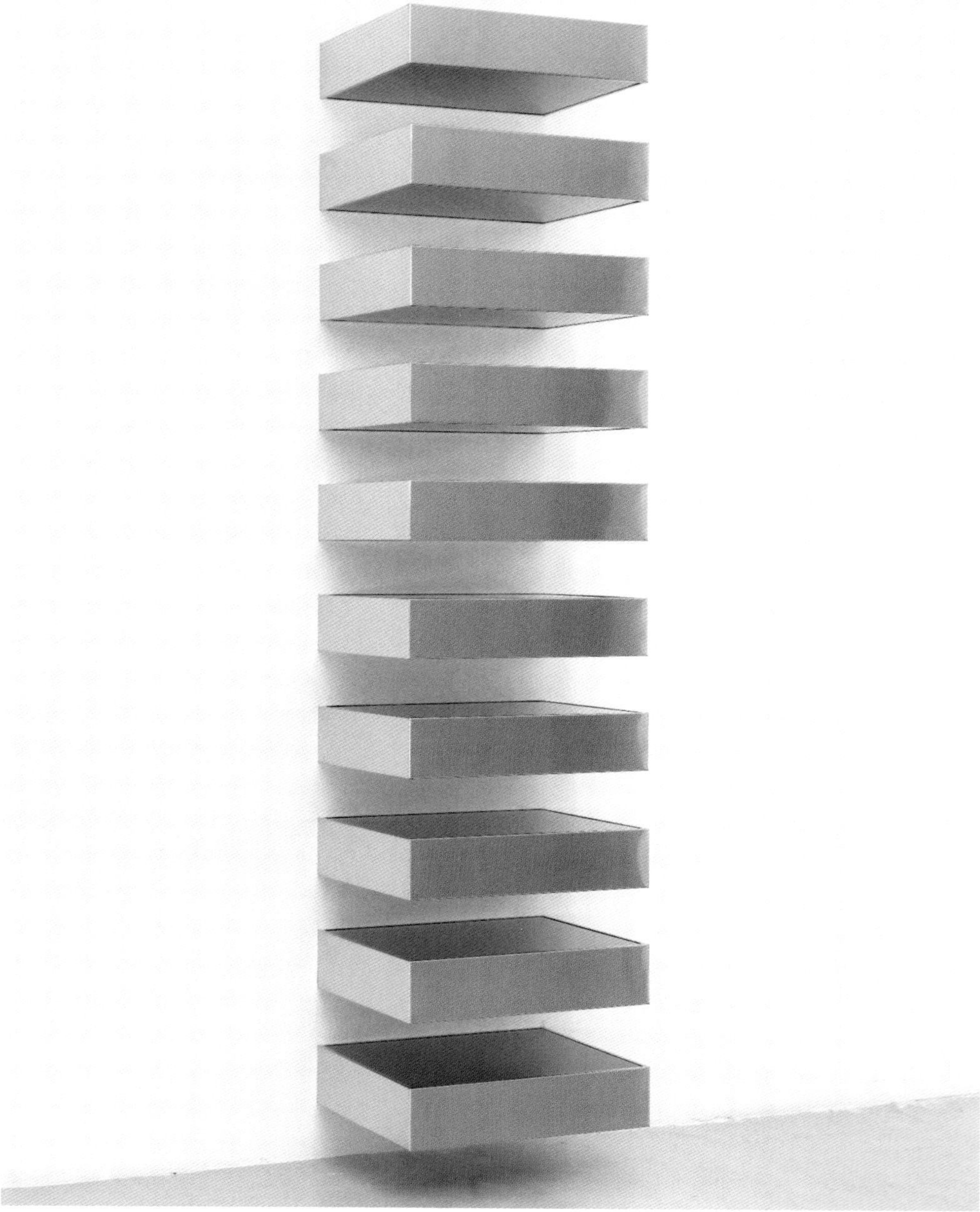

Untitled, 1992, stainless steel, plexiglass, 10 units, each 6 1/8" x 24" x 27"

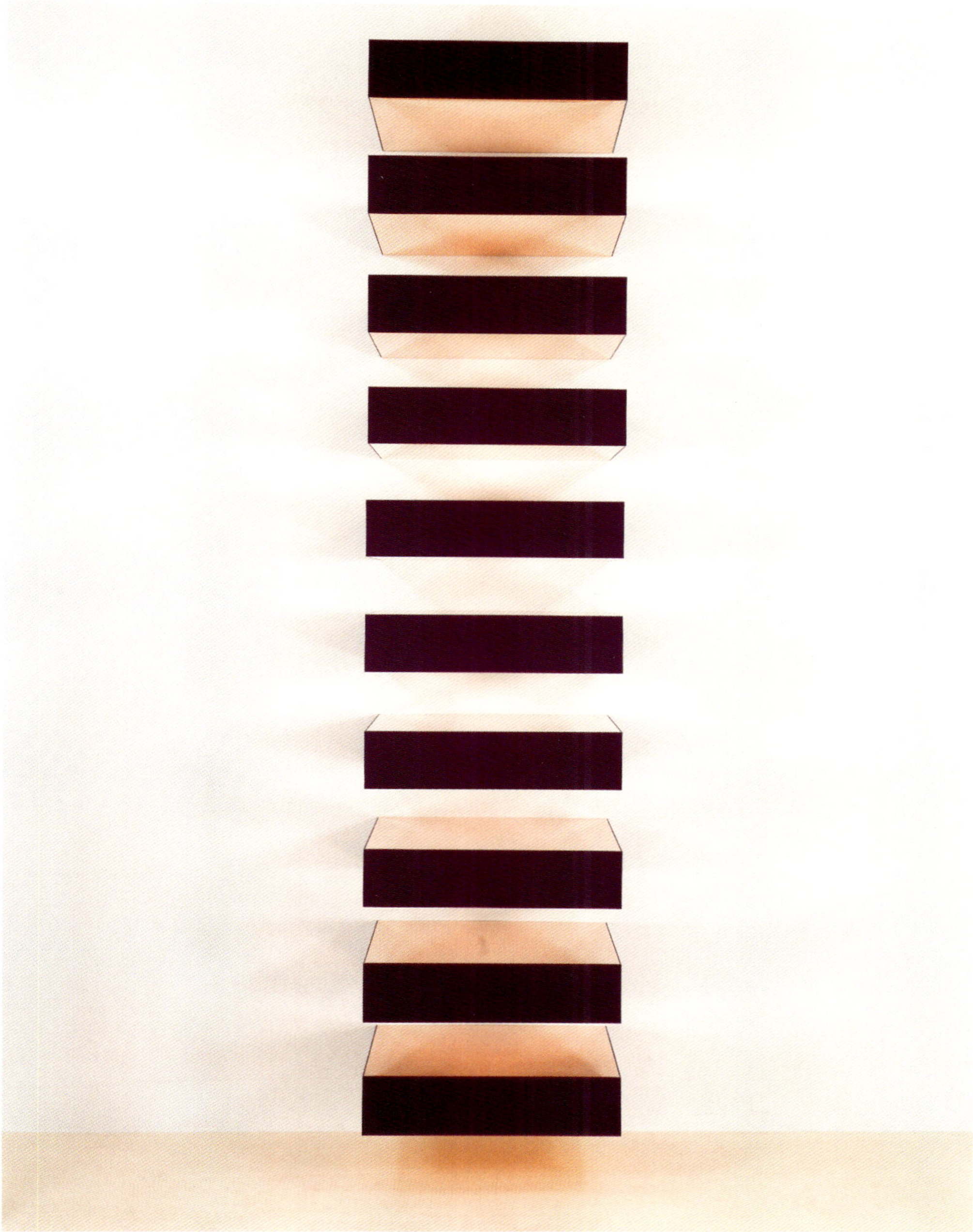

Untitled, 1993, copper with wrap around plexiglass, 10 units, each 9 7/8" x 39 3/4" x 30 1/2" (cat. no. 27)

Bruder Frank in Hamburg, built from 1929 to 1931. The greatest diversity built deliberately and at once that I have seen is the *Zeche Zollverein* near Essen, built in the early '30s. But, like color, diversity disappeared in commercialism, even when the money was public.

Primarily diversity should be produced by the plan of the streets and buildings, which make the fundamental structure, which includes the questions of where to live, to work, go to school, and where to ignore art and music. But secondarily, not just as decoration, not even as large decoration, not even as a parallel activity, color should be part of the necessary diversity. In architecture color is part of architecture; it isn't part of art. The integrity of each is damaged by being mixed. In the *Gesamtkunstwerk* more is less.

Itten wrote in 1916: "Form is also color. Without color there is no form. Form and color are one." It never occured to me to make three-dimensional work without color. I took Itten's premise, which I had not read, for granted. Sculpture itself was a distant idea to me, that it be only white or gray was a notion of the academy. This is why so much of this essay is about space. Color and space occur together. I consider black, gray, and white to be color, as Leonardo did, despite, as he says, philosophers, and despite Mondrian and van Doesburg. Aside from the scientific view of light as color and its absence as the absence of color, which is true of course, it is also true that the whole range from white through the colors to black can be seen in light. Color as the spectrum and color as material, so to speak, are not the same. Black can be seen in the light. And also, again, all materials, gray and tan, are colored.

I did not study sculpture; I studied painting and made paintings until 1961. I liked David Smith's sculpture but considered it a very different aspect of art. Sculpture in North America never reached the invention of painting. Even Smith's work was somewhat backward, backward even in relation to the sculpture by Arp, although he was older. Tony Smith's supposed influence is an instance of the ignorance of chronology. The first work that I saw of his was two 4 x 4 x 8 foot black boxes which were separate but could be placed together to form a cube. These were plywood mock-ups for welded metal. This was in March 1964 at the Wadsworth Athenaeum. The work was not interesting and the black contradicted, by making vague, the volume of the work. Before 1964 Smith was known only as a friend of Pollock and Newman and as an architect on Long Island. The three-dimensional work that I began 1962 was new and the complete use of color was new.

While I was making the first two works and the right angle I realized that there had been no such work before. I was puzzled by them, especially the first, the relief that isn't a relief. I had made what I wanted. The paintings were difficult: each one had aspects that I wanted and aspects that I didn't, usually opposed.

The three-dimensional work eliminated or solved the contradictions. For example, the paintings were large rectangles of color, usually cadmium red light, with lines, painted or sometimes incised. The lines, cut or not, were an element on top of the rectangle. The breadth of the colored rectangle and the narrowness of the lines could never become only one element, one whole. The right angle and the subsequent rectangular volumes on the floor, all the same red, were large planes, more than one, whose edges were definite lines. Their edges were not the boundaries of one plane on a wall but were the quiet transition from one plane to another, quiet but more definite than the boundaries, since it was undeniable that they were at 90 degrees to each other. The new work seemed to be the beginning of my own freedom, with possibilities for a lifetime. The possibilities and the lifetime are now well along.

The narrow and lazy nature of art criticism makes it difficult to know the diversity of my work, or of anyone's, but if the list of exhibitions at the back of the catalog is related to what the exhibitions contained, the diversity is obvious and the substantial prior invention proven.

In 1904 Julius Meier-Graefe wrote: "The incomprehensibility of painting and sculpture to the general public has been shrouded in a veil of pretentious exposition." All of the works in the many exhibitions were difficult and expensive to construct. Artists are not supposed to think about money, but I paid for the work, either directly or finally because an advance was a debt to the gallery. To construct work in three dimensions is to be damned to ambivalence within the society. I had intended to be like Albert Pinkham Ryder, working quietly and cheaply alone. Almost all of the best work now is three-dimensional, as I said before. I don't see how the artists can pay for their work; which means, how can art continue? The situation seems hopeless.

To repeat in some detail, color and three-dimensional space were placed directly on the floor, as one. Neither existed before. A direct relationship to the supporting structure had not existed before. Despite some geometric painting in New York related to Mondrian, which was ignored, despite Albers and Reinhardt, who were disparaged, despite Noland, who was praised, the geometry, color, space, and the relationship to the support were completely new. My attitude toward geometry was new. It was not at all related to Mondrian's attitude, which was so clear and developed, like red, yellow, blue, and white, that I long thought that all geometry belonged to Mondrian. Geometry and mathematics are human inventions. I use a small, simple portion in my work for my purposes. Four units in a row are only that. They are not part of infinity, either endless or above or within. They are a small, finite order that I am interested in. They are not the turtle that supports the world. There are a lot of rectangles in the world and one that I have made exists as one of them. The idea of a rectangle exists only as an idea, which is easy for rectangles and difficult for most ideas. The idea of an automobile becomes uncertain; the idea of the society can't be clarified as an idea; the idea of the universe is pretty much a collection of facts. This is why Plato proposed the Forms.

When I was making the paintings and the first three-dimensional works I knew how far I had to go and how new the work had to be to be my own. Pollock, Newman, Mondrian, and all first-rate artists establish that distance. The negative force, like Locke's "uneasiness," is that it is not possible to understand borrowed colors and forms sufficiently to make new first-rate work. Many artists in the '60s and at the present think that it is enough to go next door, even to the neighbors. Some in New York in the '60s looked at Pollock and the others and made passable work for a few years and then once secure did what they wanted to do in the first place, as did Warhol, or they didn't know what to do, as Stella doesn't. They were made by the high situation in New York and then they helped to destroy it, which in general is the story of art appreciation in New York. Earlier, for example, but better, the work of Guston and Kline was made by the situation. Most work was not unusual enough to be anyone's; most was not sufficient. It was not enough to vary the predictable; it was not enough to renovate old brushwork.

Pollock, Newman, Rothko, and Still were the best artists and could not be matched in painting, which therefore could not continue at that level. Noland and especially Louis are good artists but their work is not equal. I didn't think when I said thirty years ago that painting was finished that it would be so thoroughly finished. The achievement of Pollock and the others meant that the century's development of color could continue no further on a flat surface. Its adventitious capacity to destroy naturalism also could not continue. Perhaps Pollock, Newman, Rothko, and Still were the last painters. I like Agnes Martin's paintings. Someday, not soon, there will be another kind of painting, far from the easel, far from beyond the easel, since our environment indoors is four walls, usually flat. Color to continue had to occur in space.

The subject of color in regard to myself and to everyone else is obviously too large for this essay. I think now that I intended to write a particular book, instead this is a general essay. I wanted to begin with Aristotle and to continue with Newton and discuss all the color theories and circles. I wanted to discuss Goethe and M. E. Chevreul, whose book I've had for thirty years, inadvertently on loan from Ed Clark, and Adolf Hoelzel, who taught at the Stuttgart Academy when Itten was a student there, who taught that colors have feelings. Like the history of the nation taught in school, which never continues beyond the glorious beginning, I would never have reached the inglorious present, in which there is my own work, which is of more interest to me. I'm going to neglect all of may work until some of 1983 which is made of aluminum sheet painted in colors.

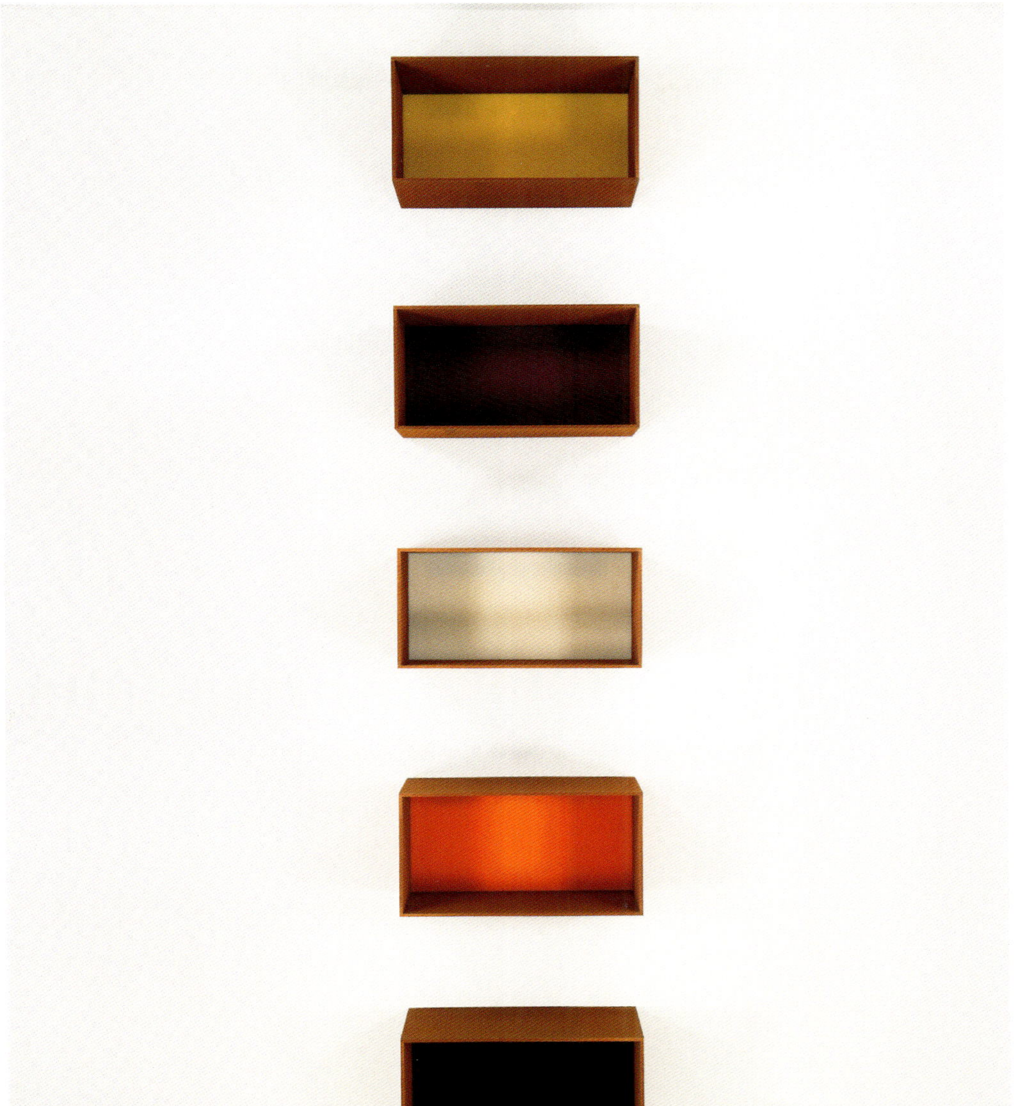

Untitled, 1992, Cor-ten steel, plexiglass, 6 units, each 19 5/8" x 39 3/4" x 19 5/8" (cat. no. 26)

Color will always be interpreted in a new way, so that I hardly think my use is final, in fact I think it is a beginning. Infinite change may be its constant nature. Color is opposite to the projection of feeling described to Goethe, Hoelzel and Itten. The idealism of Mondrian is very different. The attitude of Albers is different again. No immediate feeling can be attributed to color. Nothing can be identified. If it seems otherwise, usually the association is cultural, for example, the light blue and white, supposedly the colors of peace, of the cops and the United Nations. If there were an identifiable feeling to red or to red and black together they would not be usable to me.

Color is like material. It is one way or another, but it obdurately exists. Its existence as it is is the main fact and not what it might mean, which may be nothing. Or rather, color does not connect alone to any of the several states of the mind. I mention the word "epistemology" and stop. Color, like material, is what art is made from. It alone is not art. Itten confused the components with the whole. Other than the spectrum, there is no pure color. It always occurs on a surface which has no texture or which has a texture or which is beneath a transparent surface.

In the sheet aluminum works I wanted to use more and diverse bright colors than before. As I will describe later, there are many combinations, some old as I listed, and some my own from earlier work. I wanted to avoid both of these. I especially didn't want the combinations to be harmonious, an old and implicative idea, which is the easiest to avoid, or to be inharmonious in reaction, which is harder to avoid. I wanted all of the colors to be present at once. I didn't want them to combine. I wanted a multiplicity all at once that I had not known before. This was very difficult. The construction of the work in panels limited the use of ratio, the extent of one color to another, but this is perhaps just as well.

After a few decades the discussion of color is so unknown that it would have to begin with a spot. How large is it? Is it on a flat surface? How large is that? What color is that? What color is the spot? Red. If a second spot is placed on the surface, what color is it? Black? What if both spots were red, or black? How far away is the black spot from the red spot? Enough for these to be two discrete spots, one red and one black? Or near enough for there to be a pair of spots, red and black? Or apart enough for this to be uncertain?

What if the red and black spots are next to each other? And of course, which red? cadmium red medium, and which black? ivory black. The red could also be cadmium red light, the medium, cadmium red dark or alizarin crimson. In a way, side by side, the red and the black become one color. They become a two-color monochrome. Red and black together are so familiar that they almost form a new unity. Every easily known color paired with either black or white forms such a monochrome: orange, yellow, blue, green. Because of the black and white, also a pair, these pairs have a somewhat flat quality, are somewhat monochromatic.

The contrasting pairs are just as well known: red and blue, red and green, red and yellow, blue and green, blue and yellow. Some are not: red and orange, yellow and orange. This list is finite, since it is of primaries and secondaries. The other possible pairs are infinite, as is color, whether in the spectrum or materially mixed. All colors of the same value, such as light yellow and light green, make pairs. All values of the same color make pairs. Full colors pair, such as cadmium red medium, cadmium orange medium, and cadmium yellow medium. A group of colors, without an adjective like "full," that I especially like is of course cadmium red light, cerulean blue, chartreuse, and permanent green. In 1964 another work on the floor was painted chartreuse with half of an inset iron pipe sprayed cream yellow, a somewhat sharp and acid color opposed to one white and full (ill. p. 23). Words to describe colors are scarce. The really acid colors, clear, sharp, and dark, are pthalocyanine blue and green. Also clear and sharp and not as dark are the seemingly stained colors like those used by El Greco: alizarin crimson, ultramarine blue, and viridian. These also occur in the Hours of Jeanne d'Évreux opposed to *grisaille*. The somewhat soft colors correspond. These are full but seem to have white mixed in them, which they don't: cadmium red medium, cadmium yellow light, emerald green, and especially cobalt blue. Dull or grayed colors, the ochres, the oxides, all form pairs, united by value. And, as in the chartreuse work, there are pairs opposed: cobalt blue and cerulean blue, cobalt blue and cadmium red light.

There are also monochromatic triads, red and black and white, and there are contrasting triads. There are sequential triads of color and value: cadmium red light, medium, and dark. And then color becomes complicated: red, black, and cadmium yellow light, medium, or dark. Then perhaps red and black and the pair (A + B) or (B + C) or (A + B) + (B + C) + (C + D) or (A + B) + (C + D) + (E + F). The schemes for the large works with colored panels are very complicated. Often they require all possible combinations of four colors or eight colors. The colors cannot touch side by side or end to end. In the work the relationships of the colors are differently intelligible. One above another they are easy to see as a pair; diagonally they are not. Basically I want the pairs and the sequences and the possibilities to be only color. The structure is part of the whole. Chaos would not achieve what I want. It requires a greater number, which if great enough becomes order. First, the parts would touch, and second, the colors would not be distributed more or less evenly. But mainly the initial selection of colors prohibits randomness. In a note of 1965 I wrote that form, which I don't like so much as a word, and color should be "intelligent without being ordered."

Color of course can be an image or a symbol, as is the peaceful blue and white, often combined with olive drab, but these are no longer present in the best art. By definition, images and symbols are made by institutions. A pair of colors that I knew of as a child in Nebraska was red and black, which a book said was the “favorite” of the Lakota. In the codices of the Maya, red and black signify wisdom and are the colors of scholars.

The painting of the generation in Europe after Mondrian and Matisse was obscured by World War II, as everything civilized is obscured by war, which is a consequence delightful to soldiers, so that continuity and the innovation of the new art was not considered. The artists who especially developed color were Olle Baertling, who also developed space in his sculpture, and Richard Paul Lohse. In the United States, where art is always obscure, partly because for the permanent military, in addition to Albers, from Bottrop, and Reinhardt, there was especially Al Jensen, from Guatemala, from among the Maya.

Untitled, 1991, Cor-ten steel, painted back, 4 units, each 39 1/4“ x 39 3/4“ x 19 5/8“

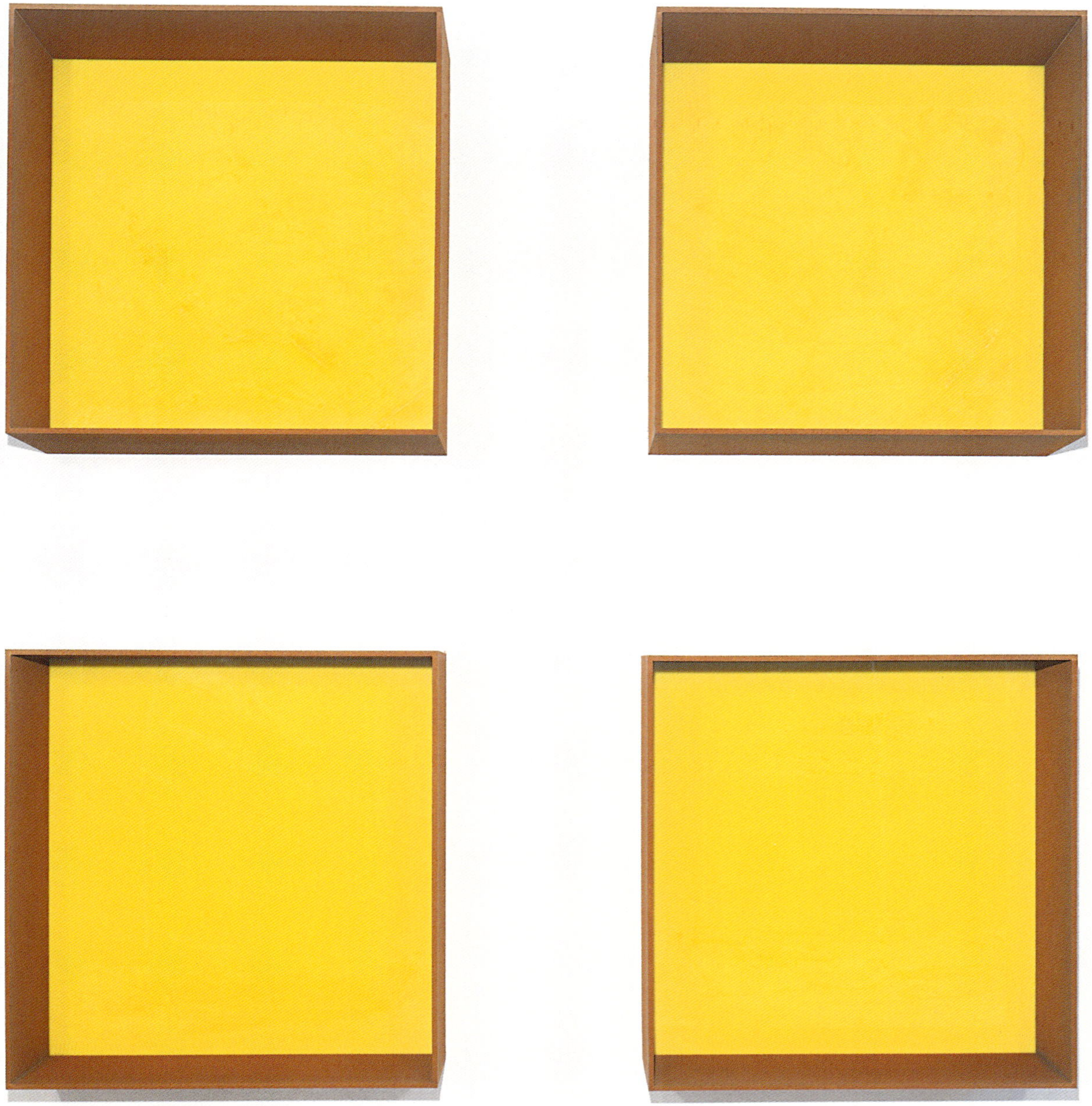

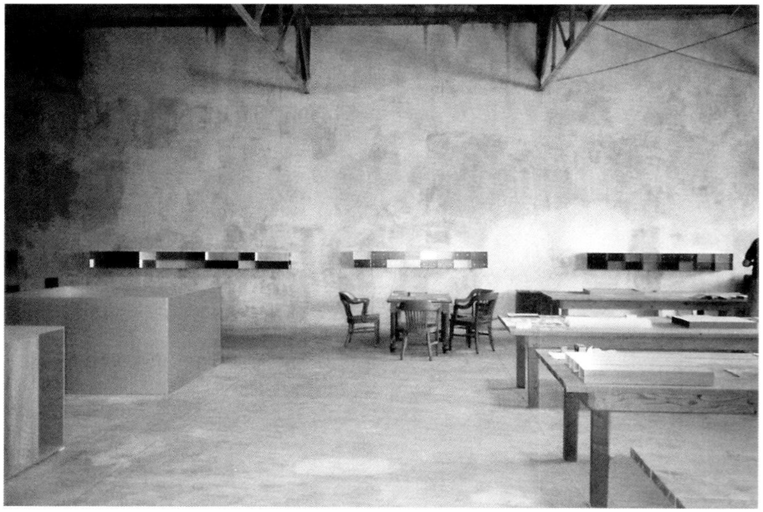

Studio, Marfa 1999

Biography

1928
Born on 3 June in Excelsior Spring, Missouri

1948/49
Studied at the College of William and Mary, Williamsburg

1948–1953
Studied at the Art Students League, New York
Studied at Columbia University, New York, qualifying in Philosophy

1957–1962
Studied Art History at Columbia University, New York

1959–1965
Art critic for various magazines

1962–1964
Taught at Brooklyn Institute of Arts and Sciences, Brooklyn, New York

1967
Taught at Yale University, New Haven

1968
Bought the building at 101 Spring Street in New York. Awarded a Guggenheim Fellowship

1971
Moved to Marfa, Texas

1976
Baldwin Professor at Oberlin College, Ohio

1986
Opening of a permanent exhibition of his works at the Chinati Foundation, Marfa

1987
Awarded the Skowhegan Medal for Sculpture by the Skowhegan School of Painting and Sculpture, Mayne, and the Brandeis University Medal for Sculpture by Brandeis University, Waltham, Massachusetts

1992
Prize from the Stankowski Foundation, Stuttgart

1993
Award from the Sikkens Foundation, Sassenheim, the Netherlands

1994
Donald Judd died on 12 February in New York

Solo Exhibitions

1957
Panoras Gallery, New York

1963
Green Gallery, New York

1966
Leo Castelli Gallery, New York

1968
Whitney Museum of American Art, New York
Irving Blum Gallery, Los Angeles

1969
Galerie Bruno Bischofberger, Zurich
Leo Castelli Gallery, New York
Structures, Galerie Ileana Sonnabend, Paris
Galerie Rudolf Zwirner, Cologne
Irving Blum Gallery, Los Angeles

1970
Stedelijk van Abbemuseum, Eindhoven;
Folkwang Museum, Essen;
Kunstverein, Hanover;
Whitechapel Art Gallery, London
The Helman Gallery, St. Louis
Leo Castelli Gallery and Warehouse, New York
Galerie Konrad Fischer, Dusseldorf
Janie C. Lee Gallery, Dallas
Drawings and Sculpture, Locksley Shea Gallery, Minneapolis

1971
Pasadena Art Museum, Pasadena
Stainless Steel Progressions, Locksley Shea Gallery, Minneapolis

1972
The Greenberg Gallery, St. Louis
Galerie Rolf Ricke, Kön
Galerie Daniel Templon, Paris
Leo Castelli Gallery, New York (with Richard Serra)

1973
Leo Castelli Gallery, New York
Galleria Sperone/Fischer, Rome
Galerie Daniel Templon, Paris
Early Works – Recent Works, Locksley Shea Gallery, Minneapolis
Galleria Gian Enzo Sperone, Turin
22 Objects, Galerie Annemarie Verna, Zurich

1974
Lisson Gallery, London
Ace Gallery, Venice, CA
Portland Center of the Visual Arts, Portland

1975
Galerie Aronowitsch, Stockholm
The National Gallery of Canada, Ottawa
Galerie Daniel Templon, Paris
Lisson Gallery, London

1976
Leo Castelli Gallery, New York

Galerie Annemarie Verna, Zurich
Skulpturen, Kunsthalle, Bern
Zeichnungen/Drawings 1956–1976, Kunstmuseum Basel;
Staatliche Kunsthalle, Tübingen;
Museum des 20. Jahrhunderts, Vienna;
Musée d'Art et d'Histoire, Geneva;
Museum of Modern Art, Oxford
Janie C. Lee Gallery, Houston
Sable-Castelli Gallery, Toronto

1977
Art Museum of South Texas, Corpus Christi, TX
Heiner Friedrich Gallery, New York
Galerie Heiner Friedrich, Cologne
Donald Judd für Josef Albers, Moderne Galerie Bottrop
Contemporary Arts Center, Cincinnati
Concrete, Ace Gallery, Venice, CA
Metal, Ace Gallery, Los Angeles

1978
Neue Nationalgalerie, Berlin
The Sculpture of Donald Judd, Watari Gallery, Tokyo
Leo Castelli Gallery, New York
Drawings 1956–76, Rijksmuseum Kröller-Müller, Otterlo
Vancouver Art Gallery, Vancouver
Galerie Heiner Friedrich, Munich
Heiner Friedrich Gallery, New York
New Work, Young-Hoffman Gallery, Chicago

1979
Survey of Work 1963–1979, Leo Castelli Gallery, New York
Stedelijk van Abbemuseum, Eindhoven
Lisson Gallery, London
Akron Art Institute, Akron
Galerie Heiner Friedrich, Cologne
Sculpture, Thomas Segal Gallery, Boston

1980
Galerie Annemarie Verna, Zurich

1981
Leo Castelli Gallery, New York
Newport Harbor Art Museum, Newport, CA

1982
Major Pieces, Larry Gagosian Gallery, Los Angeles

1983
Leo Castelli Gallery, New York
Galerie Annemarie Verna, Zurich
Carol Taylor Art, Dallas
Eight Works in Three Dimensions, Knight Gallery, Spirit Square Art Center, Charlotte
Early Works, BlumHelman Gallery, New York
Furniture by Donald Judd, 101 Spring Street, New York
Margo Leavin Gallery, Los Angeles
Leo Castelli Gallery, New York
Furniture, Max Protech Gallery, New York

1985
Skulpturen, Galerie Annemarie Verna, Zurich
Galleria Lia Rumma, Naples
Texas Gallery, Houston
Galerie Bärbel Grässlin, Frankfurt/M.
Sculpture/Furniture, Rhona Hoffman Gallery, Chicago

1986
Waddington Galleries, London
Paula Cooper Gallery, New York

1987
Galerie Rolf Ricke, Cologne
Margo Leavin Gallery, Los Angeles
Lawrence Olivier Gallery, Philadelphia
Galerie Maeght Lelong, Paris
Stedelijk van Abbemuseum, Eindhoven;
Städtische Kunsthalle, Dusseldorf;
ARC/Musée d'Art Moderne de la Ville de Paris;
Fundació Joan Miró, Barcelona
Adair Margo Gallery, El Paso
Galerie Annemarie Verna, Zurich

1988
Castello di Rivoli, Turin
Galerie nächst St. Stephan, Vienna
Galerie Aronowitsch, Stockholm
Whitney Museum of American Art, New York
Vivian Horan Fine Art, New York
Galerie Lelong, New York (with Robert Mangold)
Furniture Architectural Studies and Sculpture, Paula Cooper Gallery, New York
Lawrence Oliver Gallery, Philadelphia
Galerie Rolf Ricke, Cologne

1989
Dallas Museum of Art, Dallas
Architektur, Westfälischer Kunstverein, Münster
Waddington Galleries, London
Donald Young Gallery, Chicago
Staatliche Kunsthalle Baden-Baden
Städtisches Museum Abteiberg, Mönchengladbach
Gallery Yamaguchi, Osaka
Margo Leavin Gallery, Los Angeles
Möbler, Galerie Aronowitsch, Stockholm
Museum of Fine Arts, Boston (with Agnes Martin)

1990
Barbara Krakow Gallery, Boston
Thomas Segal Gallery, Boston
Brooke Alexander Gallery, New York
Galerie Jean Bernier, Athens
Galerie Annemarie Verna, Zurich
Prints, Gallery Yamaguchi, Osaka
Kunstverein St. Gallen
Paula Cooper Gallery, New York
Soviet Cultural Foundation, Moscow
Persons & Lindell Galerie, Helsinki

1991
Galerie Rolf Ricke, Cologne
Architektur, MAK, Österreichisches Museum für angewandte Kunst, Vienna
Furniture, The Saint Louis Art Museum, St. Louis
Inkong Gallery, Seoul
Galerie Ryszard Varisella, Frankfurt/M.
Galeria Theospacio, Madrid
Galerie Jean Bernier, Athens
Victoria Miro Gallery, London
The Pace Gallery, New York
Galerie Lelong, Paris

1992
Galerie Meert-Rihoux, Brussels
Blue Star Art Space, San Antonio, TX
Galerie Tanit, Munich
New Works 1991, Edition Schellmann, Munich
New Works 1991, Edition Schellmann, New York
Galerie Annemarie Verna, Zurich
Inkong Gallery, Seoul
Gallery Yamaguchi, Osaka;
Shizuoka Prefectural Museum of Art, Shizouka, Japan
Furniture, Kasseler Kunstverein, Kassel
Texas Gallery, Houston

1993
Kitakyushu Municipal Museum of Art, Kitakyushu, Japan
Large-Scale Works, The Pace Gallery, New York
Furniture Retrospective, Museum Boijmans Van Beuningen, Rotterdam;
Villa Stuck, München
Drawings – Woodblocks, Galerie Meert-Rihoux, Brussels
Margo Leavin Gallery, Los Angeles (with John Chamberlain)
Prints 1951–1993, Haags Gemeentemuseum, The Hague
Stedelijk Museum, Amsterdam
Kunst + Design, Museum Wiesbaden

1994
Kunst + Design, Städtische Kunstsammlungen, Chemnitz;
Badisches Landesmuseum, Karlsruhe
The Moscow Installation, Galerie Gmurzynska, Cologne
The Last Editions, Brooke Alexander Editions, New York
Sculpture, The Pace Gallery, New York
Galerie Annemarie Verna, Zurich

1995
Sculpture 1963–1990, Paula Cooper Gallery, New York
Gallery Seomi, Seoul
Furniture, A/D Gallery, New York
Wall Pieces by Donald Judd, The Chinati Foundation, Marfa, TX
Galerie Walcheturm, Zurich
Sculpture, Furniture, Prints Architecture, The Museum of Modern Art, Oxford;
Kunsthallen Brandts Klaefabrik, Odense

1996
Furniture, Prints, Sculpture, Barbara Krakow Gallery, Boston
Graphic Works, Galleri Weinberger, Copenhagen
PaceWildenstein Gallery, Los Angeles
Drawings, Susan Inglett Gallery, New York
Furniture, The Parrish Art Museum, Southampton
Kent Gallery, New York (with Richard Artschwager)
Retrospektive der Druckgraphik, Museum Wiesbaden

1997
Escultura, Gravura, Mobiliario, Centro Cultural de Belem, Lisbon
Furniture, PaceWildenstein Gallery, Los Angeles
Concrete Work, The Sculpture Garden, New York
Woodcuts and Sculpture, Brooke Alexander Editions, New York
60's Works, Faggionato Fine Arts, London
Galerie Xavier Hufkens, Brussels
Galerie Bugdahn und Kaimer, Dusseldorf
Large Scale Works from the Donald Judd Estate, Marfa, Texas, Lisson Gallery, London
Galeria Ramis Barquet, Monterey, Mexico

1998
Sculpture and Early Woodcuts, Paula Cooper Gallery, New York
Early Fabricated Work, PaceWildenstein Gallery, New York
Galerie Annemarie Verna, Zurich
A Good Chair is a Good Chair. The Furniture of Donald Judd, The Contemporary Arts Center, Cincinnati
Aspects of Color, The Menil Collection, Houston (with Dan Flavin)

1999
Selected Works 1960–1991, The Museum of Modern Art, Saitama; The Museum of Modern Art, Shiga

2000
Donald Judd. Colorist, Sprengel Museum Hannover;
Kunsthaus Bregenz

Bibliography (selection)

Writings by Donald Judd

Donald Judd's texts until 1986 are available in two collected volumes:

Complete Writings 1959–1975, Halifax/New York 1975.

Complete Writings 1975–1986, Stedelijk van Abbemuseum, Eindhoven 1987.

Bilderstreit, in: *Art & Design,* July /Aug. 1989, p. 51/52.

Kunst und Architektur, 1987, in: *Donald Judd. Architektur* (cat.), Westfälischer Kunstverein, Münster 1989, pp. 167–172 (English text pp. 194–199).

In Ergänzung, in: Donald Judd. *Architektur* (cat.), Westfälischer Kunstverein, Münster 1989, pp. 200–203 (English text pp. 207– 209).

Una Stanza per Panza, Part I, in: *Kunst Intern,* No. 4, May/June 1990, pp. 13–21.

Una Stanza per Panza, Part II, in: *Kunst Intern,* No. 5, July/Aug. 1990, pp. 72–77.

Una Stanza per Panza, Part III, in: *Kunst Intern,* No. 6, Sept./Oct. 1990, pp. 89–95.

Una Stanza per Panza, Part IV, in: *Kunst Intern,* No. 7, Nov./Dec. 1990, pp. 93–99.

Josef Albers, in: *Josef Albers* (cat.), The Chinati Foundation, Marfa 1991, pp. 7–25.

21 February 93, in: Donald Judd. *Large-Scale Works* (cat.), The Pace Gallery, New York 1993, pp. 9–13.

It's hard to find a good lamp, in: *Donald Judd. Furniture Retrospective* (cat.), Museum Boijmans Van Beuningen, Rotterdam 1993, pp. 7–21 (Text in Dutch, English and German).

Eichholteren, Switzerland, in: *Donald Judd. Furniture Retrospective* (cat.), Museum Boijmans Van Beuningen, Rotterdam 1993, p. 99 (Text in Dutch, English and German).

Marfa, Texas – Concrete Buildings, in: *Donald Judd. Furniture Retrospective* (cat.), Museum Boijmans Van Beuningen, Rotterdam 1993, p. 103 (Text in Dutch, English and German).

101 Spring Street, New York City, in: *Donald Judd. Furniture Retrospective* (cat.), Museum Boijmans Van Beuningen, Rotterdam 1993, pp. 109–113 (Text in Dutch, English and German).

Some aspects of color in general and red and black in particular, Sikkens Foundation, Sassenheim/ Stedelijk Museum Amsterdam, 1993.

Interviews

Bruce Glaser: *Questions to Stella and Judd,* in: *Artnews,* Sept. 1966, pp. 55–61.

John Coplans: *An Interview with Donald Judd,* in: *Artforum,* June 1971, pp. 45/47.

Jean-Claude Lebensztejn: *Eight Statements. Donald Judd,* in: *Art in America,* July/Aug. 1975, pp. 71/72.

Paul Taylor: *Interview with Donald Judd,* in: *Flash Art,* May 1987, pp. 35–37.

Jose Lebrero Stals: *Interview with Donald Judd,* in: *Lapiz,* No. 44, 1988, p. 16.

David Batchelor: *A Small Kind of Order: Donald Judd,* in: *Artscribe International,* Nov./Dec. 1989, pp. 62–67.

John Griffiths: *Donald Judd,* in: *Art & Design,* July/Aug. 1989, pp. 47–49.

Jochen Poetter: *Zurück zur Klarheit. Gespräch mit Donald Judd* (Interview), in: *Donald Judd* (cat.), Staatliche Kunsthalle Baden-Baden, 1989, pp. 65–86 (English text pp. 87–104).

Angeli Janhsen u. a.: *Gespräch mit Donald Judd* (Interview), in: *Donald Judd* (cat.), Kunstverein St. Gallen, 1990, pp. 39–47 (English text pp. 50–56).

Todd Eberle: *Donald Judd. The Interview,* in: *Interview,* April 1994, pp. 90–99.

Texts on Donald Judd

Barbara Rose: *Donald Judd,* in: *Artforum,* June 1965, pp. 30–32.

Barbara Rose: *ABC Art,* in: *Art in America,* Oct./Nov. 1965, pp. 57–69.

Robert Smithson: *Donald Judd,* in: *7 Sculptors* (cat.), Institute of Contemporary Art, Philadelphia 1965, pp. 21–23.

Robert Smithson: *The Crystal Land,* in: *Harper's Bazaar,* May 1966, pp. 72/73.

Rosalind Krauss: *Allusion and Illusion in Donald Judd,* in: *Artforum,* May 1966, pp. 24–26.

William C. Agee: *Don Judd,* in: *Donald Judd* (cat.), Whitney Museum of American Art, New York 1968, unpag.

Elisabeth C. Baker: *Judd the Obscure,* in: *Art in America,* April 1968, pp. 44/45, 60–62.

Roelof Louw: *Judd and After,* in: *Studio International,* Nov. 1972, pp. 171–175.

Rosalind Krauss: *Sense and Sensibility. Reflections on Post '60s Sculpture,* in: *Artforum,* Nov. 1973, pp. 43–52.

Roberta Smith: *Donald Judd,* in: *Donald Judd* (Catalogue Raisonné), National Gallery of Canada, Ottawa 1975, pp. 3–33.

William C. Agee: *Unit, Series, Site: A Judd Lexicon,* in: *Art in America,* May/June 1975, pp. 40–49.

Dieter Koepplin: *Vorwort,* in: *Donald Judd. Zeichnungen/Drawings 1956–1976* (cat.), Kunstmuseum Basel, 1976, pp. 3–7 (English text pp. 8–12).

Phyllis Tuchman: *Minimalism and Critical Response,* in: *Artforum,* May 1977, pp. 26–31.

Kenneth Baker: *Donald Judd: Past Theory,* in: *Artforum,* Summer 1977, pp. 46/47.

Roberta Smith: *Multiple Returns,* in: *Art in America,* March 1982, pp. 112–114.

Prudence Carlson: *Donald Judd's Equivocal Objects,* in: *Art in America,* January 1984, pp. 114–118.

Rainer Crone: *Symmetrie und Ordnung. Die formale Logik in Donald Judds Skulpturen,* in: *Donald Judd* (cat.), Stedelijk van Abbemuseum, Eindhoven 1987, pp. 61–75 (Text in German and English).

Germano Celant: *Donald Judd,* in: *Artstudio,* Autumn 1987, pp. 68–83.

Catherine Millet: *La petite logique de Donald Judd,* in: *Art Press,* Nov. 1987, pp. 4–10.

Barbara Haskell: *Donald Judd: Beyond Formalism,* in: *Donald Judd* (cat.), Withney Museum of American Art, New York 1988, pp. 17–114, 147–151.

Barbara Haskell: *The Vision Extended: Marfa, Texas,* in: *Donald Judd* (cat.), Whitney Museum of American Art, New York 1988, pp. 117–124, 151.

John Yau: *Donald Judd,* in: *Contemporanea,* March/April 1989, pp. 58–60.

Jochen Poetter: *Hermetik und Offenheit – Präzision und Schönheit. Donald Judd in der Kunsthalle Baden-Baden,* in: *Donald Judd* (cat.), Staatliche Kunsthalle Baden-Baden, 1989, pp. 7–32 (English text pp. 33–50).

Franz Meyer: *„Specific objects", Minimal Art und Don Judd,* in: *Donald Judd* (cat.), Staatliche Kunsthalle Baden-Baden, 1989, pp. 51–57 (English text pp. 58–64).

Jochen Poetter: *Zurück zur Klarheit. Gespräch mit Donald Judd,* in: *Donald Judd* (cat.), Staatliche Kunsthalle Baden-Baden, 1989, pp. 65–86 (English text pp. 87–104).

Renate Puvogel: *Dan Flavin und Donald Judd in der Kunsthalle Baden-Baden,* in: *Parkett,* No. 22, 1989, pp. 14–17 (English text pp. 20–23).

Lynne Cooke: *Minimalism reviewed,* in: *The Burlington Magazine,* Sept. 1989, pp. 641–645.

Marianne Stockebrand: *Vorwort,* in: *Donald Judd. Architektur* (cat.), Westfälischer Kunstverein, Münster 1989, pp. 5–7 (English text pp. 8/9).

Lynne Cooke: *Donald Judd: Re-ordering Order,* in: *Donald Judd* (cat.), Waddington Galleries, London 1989, pp. 5–10.

Roland Wäspe: *Zur Ausstellung,* in: *Donald Judd* (cat.), Kunstverein St. Gallen, 1990, pp. 4/5 (English text pp. 6/7).

Yve-Alain Bois: *The Inflection,* in: *Donald Judd. New Sculpture* (cat.), The Pace Gallery, New York 1991, unpag.

Charles Reeve: *Cold Metal: Donald Judd's Hidden Historicity,* in: *Art History,* Dec. 1992, pp. 486–504.

Renate Puvogel: *Über Donald Judd,* in: *Donald Judd. Künstler. Kritisches Lexikon der Gegenwartskunst,* Munich 1993, pp. 3–11.

Volker Rattemeyer: *Donald Judd – Preisträger der Stankowski-Stiftung 1993,* in: *Kunst + Design. Donald Judd. Preisträger der Stankowski-Stiftung 1993* (cat.), Museum Wiesbaden, 1993, pp. 8–10 (English text pp. 11–13).

Franz Meyer: *Marfa,* in: *Kunst + Design. Donald Judd. Preisträger der Stankowski-Stiftung 1993* (cat.), Museum Wiesbaden, 1993, pp. 24–30 (English text pp. 30–36).

Renate Petzinger: *Spezifische Elemente der Architektur von Donald Judd,* in: *Kunst + Design. Donald Judd. Preisträger der Stankowski-Stiftung 1993* (cat.), Museum Wiesbaden, 1993, pp. 128–131 (English text pp. 131–134).

Rudi Fuchs: *Anstand und Schönheit,* in: *Kunst + Design. Donald Judd. Preisträger der Stankowski-Stiftung 1993* (cat.), Museum Wiesbaden, 1993, pp. 81/82 (English text pp. 83/84).

Brigitte Huck: *The Furniture,* in: *Donald Judd. Furniture Retrospective* (cat.), Museum Boijmans Van Beuningen, Rotterdam 1993, pp. 89–97 (Text in Dutch, English and German).

Rudi Fuchs: *Decent Beauty,* in: *Donald Judd. Large-Scale Works* (cat.), The Pace Gallery, New York 1993, pp. 5–7.

Richard Serra: *Donald Judd, 1928–1994,* in: *Parkett,* No. 40/41, 1994, pp. 178/179 (English text pp. 176/177).

William C. Agee: *Donald Judd in Retrospect: An Appreciation,* in: *Donald Judd. Sculpture* (cat.), The Pace Gallery, New York 1994, pp. 5–17.

Rudi Fuchs: *Meister der Farbe,* in: *Donald Judd. The Moscow Installation* (cat.), Galerie Gmurzynska, Cologne 1994, pp. 8/9 (English text pp. 10/11).

Mariette Josephus Jitta: *On Series,* in: *Donald Judd. Prints and Works in Editions. A Catalogue Raisonné,* Edition Schellmann, Munich/New York 1996, pp. 24–29 (German text pp. 37–42).

Adrian Jolles: *Eichholteren,* in: *Donald Judd Eichholteren,* Kunsthaus Bregenz (Archiv Kunst Architektur, Werkdokumente), 1997, S. 7–10 (English text pp. 15–17).

Adrian Meyer: *Metamorphose,* in: *Donald Judd Eichholteren,* Kunsthaus Bregenz (Archiv Kunst Architektur, Werkdokumente), 1997, pp. 11–14 (English text pp. 18–21).

Brydon E. Smith: (untitled), in: *Donald Judd* (cat.), Paula Cooper Gallery, New York 1995, unpag.

Rosalind E. Krauss: *The Material Uncanny,* in: *Donald Judd. Early Fabricated Work* (cat.), PaceWildenstein Gallery, New York 1998, pp. 7–13.

Marianne Stockebrand: (untitled), in: *Dan Flavin/Donald Judd. Aspects of Color* (fold-out), The Menil Collection, Houston 1998, unpag.

Gen Umezu: *The Purification of Experiences – On the Art of Donald Judd,* in: *Donald Judd. Selected Works 1960–1991* (cat.), The Museum of Modern Art, Saitama 1999, pp. 82–87 (Japanese text pp. 69–81).

Sachiko Osaki: *Where Should a Work of Art Belong? – On the Installations by Donald Judd,* in: *Donald Judd. Selected Works 1960–1991* (cat.), The Museum of Modern Art, Saitama 1999, pp. 93–96 (Japanese text pp. 89–92).

Marianne Stockebrand: *The Chinati Foundation – A Museum Created by Donald Judd,* in: *Donald Judd. Selected Works 1960–1991* (cat.), The Museum of Modern Art, Saitama 1999, pp. 132–139 (Japanese text pp. 121–130).

List of Exhibited Works

1
Untitled, 1962/1991
Douglas Fir plywood, painted, sand, glass
46 $^{1}/_{2}$“ x 46 $^{1}/_{2}$“ x 4“
Courtesy PaceWildenstein
(Ill. p. 10)

2
Untitled, 1962/1987
Douglas Fir plywood, painted
19 $^{1}/_{2}$“ x 45“ x 30 $^{1}/_{2}$“
Louisiana Museum of Modern Art, Humlebaek, Denmark
(Exhibited only in Hanover)
(Ill. p. 18)

3
Untitled, 1968
Lacquer on galvanized iron
5“ x 69“ x 9“
Froehlich Collection, Stuttgart
(Ill. p. 29)

4
Untitled, 1968/1991
Douglas Fir plywood, painted
19 $^{1}/_{2}$“ x 45“ x 30 $^{1}/_{2}$“
Louisiana Museum of Modern Art, Humlebaek, Denmark (Exhibited only in Hanover)
(Ill. p. 19)

5
Untitled, 1969
Galvanized iron
5“ x 69“ x 8 $^{1}/_{2}$“
Private collection, Cologne
(Ill. p. 25)

6
Untitled, 1969
Clear anodized aluminum, plexiglas
33“ x 68“ x 48“
Collection Thomas and Cristina Bechtler , Switzerland
(Ill. p. 41)

7
Untitled, 1969
Lacquer on anodized aluminum
6 $^{1}/_{8}$“ x 110 $^{3}/_{4}$“ x 6“
Louisiana Museum of Modern Art, Humlebaek, Denmark
(Ill. p. 37)

8
Untitled, 1985
Enameled aluminum
11 $^{7}/_{8}$“ x 35 $^{1}/_{2}$“ x 11 $^{7}/_{8}$“
Collection Dr. H. R. Meyer, Zurich
(Ill. p. 59)

9
Untitled, 1985
Enameled aluminum
11 $^{7}/_{8}$“ x 118“ x 11 $^{7}/_{8}$“
Tate Gallery, London, presented by Janet Wolfson de Botton, 1996
(Ill. p. 61)

10
Untitled, 1985
Enameled aluminum
11 $^{7}/_{8}$“ x 59“ x 11 $^{7}/_{8}$“
Collection Lilott and Eric Berganus, Hamburg
(Ill. p. 57)

11
Untitled, 1987
Enameled aluminum
2 units, each 11 $^{7}/_{8}$“ x 141 $^{1}/_{2}$“ x 11 $^{7}/_{8}$“
Galerie Lelong, Paris
(Ill. p. 65)

12
Untitled, 1988
Aluminum, plexiglass
9 $^{7}/_{8}$“ x 39 $^{3}/_{4}$“ x 9 $^{7}/_{8}$“
Donald Judd Estate
(Ill. p. 85)

13
Untitled, 1989
Enameled aluminum
11 $^{7}/_{8}$“ x 70 $^{7}/_{8}$“ x 11 $^{7}/_{8}$“
Donald Judd Estate, courtesy PaceWildenstein
(Ill. p. 70)

14
Untitled, 1989
Enameled aluminum
11 $^{7}/_{8}$“ x 70 $^{7}/_{8}$“ x 11 $^{7}/_{8}$“
Galerie Rolf Ricke, Cologne
(Ill. p. 69)

15
Untitled, 1989
Enameled aluminum
11 $^{7}/_{8}$“ x 70 $^{7}/_{8}$“ x 11 $^{7}/_{8}$“
Sprengel Museum Hannover
(Ill. p. 71)

16
Untitled, 1989
Anodized aluminum, plexiglass
6 units, each 9 $^{7}/_{8}$“ x 19 $^{5}/_{8}$“ x 9 $^{7}/_{8}$“
Sprengel Museum Hannover, on permanent loan from the HANNOVER Rück-Stiftung
(Ill. p. 83)

17
Untitled, 1989
Cor-ten steel, plexiglass
4 units, each 9 $^{7}/_{8}$“ x 19 $^{5}/_{8}$“ x 9 $^{7}/_{8}$“
Hamburger Kunsthalle, on loan from a private collection
(Ill. p. 78)

18
Untitled, 1989
Anodized aluminum, plexiglass
39 $^{3}/_{4}$“ x 79 $^{1}/_{2}$“ x 39 $^{3}/_{4}$“
Annemarie Verna Galerie, Zurich
(Ill. pp. 94, 95)

19
Untitled, 1989
Anodized aluminum
39 $^{3}/_{4}$“ x 79 $^{1}/_{2}$“ x 39 $^{3}/_{4}$“

Annemarie Verna Galerie, Zurich
(Ill. pp. 96, 97)

20
Untitled, 1990
Stainless steel, plexiglas
10 units, each 9 7/8“ x 39 3/4“ x 30 1/2“
Donald Judd Estate
(Exhibited only in Bregenz)
(Ill. p. 107)

21
Untitled, 1991
Anodized aluminum
9 7/8“ x 39 3/4“ x 9 7/8“
Donald Judd Estate

22
Untitled, 1991
Aluminum, anodized aluminum, plexiglass
9 7/8“ x 39 3/4“ x 9 7/8“
Donald Judd Estate
(Ill. p. 87)

23
Untitled, 1991
Aluminum, transparent yellow over red plexiglass
9 7/8“ x 39 3/4“ x 9 7/8“
Donald Judd Estate
(Ill. p. 89)

24
Untitled, 1991
Aluminum, anodized aluminum, transparent blue over red plexiglass
9 7/8“ x 39 3/4“ x 9 7/8“
Donald Judd Estate
(Ill. p. 86)

25
Untitled, 1991
Aluminum, transparent yellow over black plexiglass
9 7/8“ x 39 3/4“ x 9 7/8“
Donald Judd Estate
(Ill. p. 88)

26
Untitled, 1992
Corten steel, plexiglass
6 units, each 19 5/8“ x 39 3/4“ x 19 5/8“
Donald Judd Estate, courtesy PaceWildenstein
(Ill. p. 113)

27
Untitled, 1993
Copper with wrap around plexiglass
10 units, each 9 7/8“ x 39 3/4“ x 30 1/2“
Private collection, courtesy PaceWildenstein
(Exhibited only in Hanover)
(Ill. p. 101)

28–37
Untitled, 1988
Set of 10 woodcuts printed in cadmium red light
Each 23 1/2“ x 31 1/2“ (paper size)
Edition number: 25
Brooke Alexander Editions, New York

38–47
Untitled, 1988
Set of 10 woodcuts printed in ultramarine blue
Each 23 1/2“ x 31 1/2“ (paper size)
Edition number: 25
Brooke Alexander Editions, New York

48–54
Untitled, 1990
Set of 7 woodcuts in yellow, red, black, green, blue and orange
Each 23 1/2“ x 31 1/2“ (paper size)
Edition number: 25
Brooke Alexander Editions, New York
(Ill. pp. 102–105)

55–58
Untitled, 1991
Set of 4 woodcuts printed in oxide of chromium
Each 26 1/4“ x 38 1/2“ (paper size)
Edition number: 25
Brooke Alexander Editions, New York

59–62
Untitled, 1992
Set of 4 woodcuts printed in venetian red
Each 26 1/4“ x 38 1/2“ (paper size)
Edition number: 25
Brooke Alexander Editions, New York

63–66
Untitled, 1991–1994
Set of 4 woodcuts printed in cadmium red light
Each 26 1/4“ x 38 1/2“ (paper size)
Edition number: 25
Brooke Alexander Editions, New York

67–70
Untitled, 1991–1994
Set of 4 woodcuts printed in cadmium yellow medium
Each 26 1/4“ x 38 1/2“ (paper size)
Edition number: 10
Brooke Alexander Editions, New York

71–74
Untitled, 1991–1994
Set of 4 woodcuts printed in ivory black
Each 26 1/4“ x 38 1/2“ (paper size)
Edition number: 15
Brooke Alexander Editions, New York

75–78
Untitled, 1991–1994
Set of 4 woodcuts printed in French ultramarine blue
Each 26 1/4“ x 38 1/2“ (paper size)
Edition number: 15
Brooke Alexander Editions, New York

79–82
Untitled, 1992–1993
Set of 10 woodcuts in black, blue, purple, red, orange, yellow and green
Each 23“ x 30 3/4“ (paper size)
Edition number: 30
Brooke Alexander Editions, New York

Lenders to the Exhibition

Brooke Alexander Editions, New York

Collection Thomas und Cristina Bechtler, Switzerland

Collection Lilott und Eric Berganus, Hamburg

Froehlich Collection, Stuttgart

Hamburger Kunsthalle

HANNOVER Rück-Stiftung, Hannover

Louisiana Museum of Modern Art, Humlebaek, Denmark

Donald Judd Estate

Galerie Lelong, Paris

Collection Dr. H. R. Meyer, Zurich

PaceWildenstein

Galerie Rolf Ricke, Cologne

Sprengel Museum Hannover

Tate Gallery, London

Annemarie Verna Galerie, Zurich

and several private collectors, who wish to remain anonymous.

Colophon

Donald Judd. Colorist is published to accompany the exhibition of the same name in the Sprengel Museum Hannover, from 16 January until 30 April 2000 and in the Kunsthaus Bregenz from 12 May until 9 July 2000.

Distribution in the US
D.A.P., Distributed Art Publishers,
155 Avenue of the Americas, Second Floor
USA-New York, N.Y. 10013-1507
Tel.: 212-627 19 99
Fax: 212-627 94 84

Catalog
Dietmar Elger

Design
Christina Hackenschuh, Saskia H. Rothfischer

Editor
Dietmar Elger

Reproductions
Kaufmann Prepress, Stuttgart

Typesetting
Weyhing digital, Ostfildern-Ruit

Production
Dr. Cantz'sche Druckerei, Ostfildern-Ruit

Published by
Hatje Cantz Publishers, Senefelderstr. 12
73760 Ostfildern-Ruit
Tel. ++711/4405-0; Fax ++711/4405-220
Internet: www.hatjecantz.de

ISBN 3-89322-878-0

Printed in Germany

Photo Credits

Courtesy PaceWildenstein: Cover, pp. 72, 109, 117
Donald Judd Estate, Marfa: pp. 6, 23, 48, 52, 60, 108
Ellen Page Wilson, courtesy PaceWildenstein: pp. 10, 113
D. James Dee, courtesy Paula Cooper Gallery, New York: pp. 14, 15, 32, 54, 55, 63, 66, 75, 93
Courtesy Louisiana Museum of Modern Art, Humlebaek, Denmark: pp. 18, 19, 37
Michael Herling / Uwe Vogt, Sprengel Museum Hannover: pp. 25, 44, 71, 83, 85–89, 120
Bert Burgemeister, Pfullingen, courtesy Froehlich Collection, Stuttgart: p. 28
Planet/Bent Ryberg, courtesy Froehlich Collection, Stuttgart: p. 29
© Tate Gallery, London, 1999: pp. 40, 61
Courtesy The Saatchi Collection, London: p. 41
Dietmar Elger, Hannover: pp. 45, 118
Best Fotografie, Hamburg: p. 57
J. P. Kuhn, Zürich: p. 59
Courtesy Galerie Lelong, Paris: pp. 64, 65
Courtesy Galerie Rolf Ricke, Cologne: p. 69
Sarah Harper Gifford, courtesy PaceWildenstein: p. 70
Stefan Rohner, courtesy Kunstmuseum St. Gallen, on loan from the Collection Schmid: p. 74
Elke Walford, Fotowerkstatt Hamburger Kunsthalle: p. 78
Philipp Schönborn, Munich: pp. 94–97
D. James Dee, courtesy Brooke Alexander Editions, New York: pp. 101–105
Courtesy Museum Wiesbaden: p. 107